THE LIVELY DEBATE
Response to *Humanae Vitae*

THE LIVELY DEBATE
Response to *Humanae Vitae*

"May the lively debate aroused by our encyclical lead to a better knowledge of God's will."
         —Pope Paul VI, August 30, 1968.

by WILLIAM H. ⌊SHANNON

A SEARCH BOOK: Sheed & Ward: New York

Nihil Obstat: Leo J. Steady, Ph.D., S.T.D., *Censor Librorum;* Imprimatur: †Robert F. Joyce, Bishop of Burlington, December 23, 1969. The Nihil Obstat and Imprimatur are official declarations that a book or pamphlet is considered to be free of doctrinal or moral error. No implication is contained therein that those who have granted the Nihil Obstat and Imprimatur agree with the contents, opinions or statements expressed.

© Sheed and Ward, Inc., 1970
Library of Congress Catalog Card Number 75-101551
Standard Book Numbers 8362-0374-7 (Library Edition) and 8362-0340-2 (Search Paperback Edition)
Manufactured in the United States of America

CONTENTS

INTRODUCTION

The cover of the April-May, 1968, issue of *The Critic* became famous almost overnight. Reprinted in a number of newspapers and magazines, it pictures a father and mother, surrounded by their eleven lively children, startled to attention as they watch their television set and hear the newscaster saying: "Today, a long-awaited announcement from the Vatican!"

On July 29, 1968, the caption of the *Critic* cover became the statement of a fact; the long-awaited announcement from the Vatican became a reality. Pope Paul VI released his encyclical on birth control.

The *Critic* cartoon brought smiles and laughter. The publication of the encyclical, *Humanae Vitae,* touched off reactions that ran the whole gamut of human emotions from joyful approval to defiant rejection, with all possible reactions in between: incredulity, anguish, silence, indifference, grim acceptance. Much of the reaction, at least as reported in the mass media, was highly critical. Indeed, Vatican circles, while anticipating that the encyclical would not be popular, were evidently unprepared for the storm of protest and disapproval that arose so quickly and so vehemently. Never before in history had a papal document been greeted with such widespread anger and bitterness—and this not primarily from those outside the Church, but from loyal members within the Church. In fact, the reactions outside the Roman Catholic communion seem to have been milder than those within. "The reaction by Roman Catholics to Pope Paul's encyclical is so strong," wrote the editor of *The Christian Century,* "that Protestants have no need to overreact to it."[1] What Pope Paul had hoped would unify the Church on an issue that seemed more and more to be dividing its members has only made the divisions clearer and deeper.

The encyclical, it would seem, came too late to heal these divisions. Had Pope Paul spoken four years before—and at that time it seemed likely that he might—his pronouncement would doubtless have been much more readily accepted, at least within the Roman Catholic Church. But during those four years while the Pope delayed his decision, the conviction that had already taken root in the minds of many Catholics continued to grow: a state of doubt existed in the Church. An increasing number of Catholic theologians, analyzing the natural law arguments traditionally advanced to defend the intrinsic evil of birth control, found them increasingly difficult to maintain. Married Catholics in large numbers, often with the encouragement of confessors, made their own decisions of conscience and came to the conclusion that there were situations in which inter-vention in intercourse was not only justified, but even necessary.

It is not surprising, then, that when the long period of official silence was finally broken by the publication of *Humanae Vitae,* a large segment of the Catholic world found itself unable to integrate its previously formed conclusion with a document that reiterated in the strongest possible terms the traditional position of the Church.

This is not to say of course, that the only reaction to the encyclical was negative. Quite the contrary. There was also strong approval voiced for the Pope's stand, especially in the highest ecclesiastical circles. Bishops' Conferences in various parts of the world expressed their loyalty to the Pope and their wholehearted acceptance of his encyclical, though some attached qualifications to their acceptance, and most acknowledged the difficulties that the papal teaching would create for the faithful. In addition, individual bishops, priests, married couples and some theologians took their stand with the

Pope, insisting that since Rome had spoken, the matter was decided.

It would be presumptuous at this time to attempt to weigh the comparative strength, numerical or otherwise, of those who supported the encyclical and those who in one way or another expressed their reservations about it. This much is clear: the encyclical has divided Catholics among themselves and from other Christian churches. It seems clear, also, that even though the encyclical has been published, the debate on contraception will continue within the Roman Catholic Church.

The intention of this book is principally historical: to show where that debate is now and how it reached its present point. The author's purpose is not to take sides, but to present the various stands that have been taken both before and after the publication of the encyclical. The literature on the subject is so extensive that any attempt to summarize it must, of necessity, be selective. It is hoped that the selections made are honestly representative and present as far as possible a balanced picture. In presenting this summary the author has given particular—though, of course, not exclusive—emphasis to the birth control issue as it developed on the American scene.

NOTES

1. The editor, *The Christian Century* (August 14, 1968).

THE LIVELY DEBATE

Response to *Humanae Vitae*

I THE BACKGROUND
OF CASTI CONNUBII

The year 1930 represents a convenient point of departure for understanding the background of the current debate on birth control
touched off by the publication of Pope Paul's encyclical, *Humanae
Vitae*. For the year 1930 brought into dramatic confrontation two
divergent attitudes on the morality of contraception: (1) a slowly
emerging attitude on the part of some Christians that there were
circumstances in which contraceptive intercourse was justifiable, and
(2) the traditional Christian attitude that contraception was always
and in all circumstances morally reprehensible. The confrontation of
these two positions on birth control found expression in two events
of 1930: (1) the *Declaration of the Lambeth Conference,* on August
15, in which the Anglican bishops officially endorsed the use of
contraceptive methods of birth control, and (2) the publication by
Pius XI, on December 31, of the encyclical *Casti Connubii* which,
in obvious reaction to the Lambeth Declaration, condemned in the
strongest possible terms all forms of artificial birth control.

In this confrontation it must be said that the weight of Christian
tradition was on the side of *Casti Connubii*. It is true that, prior
to 1930, there had been individuals and organized groups who had
defended, loudly and vehemently, the moral acceptability of birth
control; but the moral consensus of the whole Western world was
against them. All Christian moral institutions—Christian states as
well as Christian churches—were united in their condemnation of

contraception. The advocates of birth control received little hearing in official circles. The significance of the *Declaration of the Lambeth Conference* in 1930 was that it marked the first official break of a Christian church with what had formerly been a united Christian front on the question of contraception. For the first time the advocates of birth control found their policies endorsed by a Christian church.

The sharp contrast between the *Declaration of Lambeth* and the encyclical of Pius XI symbolized what the debate on birth control was to become in the years following 1930—a debate that would find Roman Catholics on one side, and steadily increasing numbers of the rest of the Christian world on the other.

In the interests of historical accuracy, however, it must be pointed out that this was not the picture from the beginning. The contemporary birth control controversy (i.e., the controversy that began in the late nineteenth and early twentieth centuries) was fought out, at least in the United States, in the arena of Protestant thought and action before it became the cause of the Protestant-Roman Catholic tension that it is today. Indeed, it is one of the ironies of history that federal and state legislation against birth control in the United States was largely the achievement of predominantly Protestant legislatures, since these laws were enacted at a time when Roman Catholics were in no position numerically to have an effective influence on legislation, whether in the Federal Government or in the states.

ANTHONY COMSTOCK

The leader of the anti birth-control movement in the United States in the late nineteenth century was not a Roman Catholic but a zealous Protestant reformer, Anthony Comstock. By any standards, Anthony Comstock was a colorful personality who left his mark on American life and institutions.[1] The most important influence in his life was religion, but it was a religion fraught with all the darkest elements of Puritanism joined with the militant spirit of the Inquisition. His religion brought him neither joy nor consolation but, instead, a deep sense of personal sin coupled with an enormous drive to purge the world of the works and influences of the Devil. During his lifetime he became, quite successfully, a one-man censor of the morals of American society.[2] His particular mission was the suppression of obscenity in all its forms.

A man of little education, a onetime grocery clerk, Anthony Comstock became and remained for many years the secretary of the New York Society for the Suppression of Vice. But his greatest fame comes from the fact that, almost singlehandedly, he prodded the United States Congress into enacting comprehensive anti-obscenity laws. So closely did he identify himself with his cause that he spoke of this legislation as "his law"; and indeed it became popularly known as the "Comstock Law," even though its official title was "An Act for the Suppression of Trade in and Circulation of Obscene Literature and Articles of Immoral Use."

The "Comstock Law," passed by Congress on March 3, 1873, forbade the mailing or advertising through the mails of anything obscene—books, pictures, letters or articles. Obscene articles included drugs, medicines or instruments for preventing birth or for producing abortion. It was also forbidden to use the mails to give information, directly or indirectly, on where, how, from whom or by what means they could be made or obtained. Part of the bill applied to the District of Columbia and was most sweeping in its provisions. It forbade the manufacture, sale or possession of articles by which conception might be prevented; furthermore, it forbade anyone to lend or give away any published information on such articles, or even to have such information in his possession. Violation of the "Comstock Law" was punishable by five years in prison or $5,000 fine or both.[3]

The passage of this legislation was a personal victory for Anthony Comstock. No less a victory was his appointment as a special agent of the Post Office for the enforcement of the new law. No one took greater relish in his work. At one point in his career he boasted that he had destroyed more than fifty tons of indecent books, 28,425 pounds of plates for printing such books, almost four million obscene pictures and 16,900 negatives for such pictures. He even credited himself with the dubious distinction of having driven fifteen people to suicide.[4] At a later date his statistics were considerably higher: "In forty-one years . . . I have convicted persons enough to fill a passenger train of sixty-one coaches . . . I have destroyed 160 tons of obscene literature."[5]

Following the example of the Federal Government, many individual states responded to the efforts of Comstock and his energetic followers and enacted similar legislation controlling in some measure the sale, promotion or prescription of contraceptives.

MARGARET HIGGINS SANGER

These laws were not to go uncontested. In 1883, a decade after the passage of the "Comstock Law," there was born in Corning, New York, a woman whose life's work and considerable energies would be devoted to the overthrow of that law and of the mentality that it embodied. The name of Margaret Higgins Sanger (1883–1966) is practically synonymous with the birth control movement in the United States. (The very term "birth control" is of her coinage.) In 1914 she founded the National Birth Control League with a monthly magazine, *The Woman Rebel;* in the same year she published a defense of birth control called *Family Limitation,* which for many years was the "bible" of the birth control movement. Nor was she content simply to write and speak about birth control. Moved by the misery and ill health caused by unwanted pregnancies among the very poor, she determined, in spite of the law, to make information on birth control methods available to as many women as she could. Drawing on her training as a nurse and the considerable information on birth control methods she had acquired in Europe, she opened in 1916 in Brooklyn, New York, the first birth control clinic in the United States. After nine days and many clients, the clinic was closed by the police under the penal law of New York State that forbade the dissemination of birth control information. She was declared guilty of violating the law and sentenced to thirty days' imprisonment.

Undaunted by this setback, she was more determined than ever to work for a change in the law—"to raise the question of birth control," as she put it, "out of the gutter of obscenity . . . into the light of intelligence and human understanding."[6] She traveled throughout the United States and the world, using every means possible to persuade the medical profession and the general public to rally to her cause. Gradually the movement she directed with such relentless energy began to win popular support.

In 1932, with the help of a number of Protestant church groups, Margaret Sanger initiated the National Committee on Federal Legislation for Birth Control. Four years later, in 1936, the cause of birth control won its most important legal victory when a United States district court upheld the right of physicians to dispense birth control information. The court held that Congress had meant only to prohibit the "immoral use" of contraceptives, and that the use of contraceptives as prescribed by a physician was not immoral. In 1939 a federal district court in Puerto Rico permitted physicians to possess contraceptives in federal territories.

The "Comstock Law," though still unrepealed, had been rendered ineffective; contraceptives were no longer legally identified with obscene material. In 1958 the final step was taken in the abandonment of any attempt to enforce the federal law when the Post Office Department announced that it would no longer ban the mailing of contraceptives if they were not destined for "immoral purposes."

THE LAMBETH DECLARATION

In the 1930's, as a result of the gradual weakening of the federal law by reinterpretation, the birth control movement achieved the legal respectability it had sought for decades. During that same period it succeeded in acquiring in some quarters a theological respectability, too. For, as was mentioned earlier, on August 15, 1930, the Anglican

Church in the Lambeth Declaration became the first Christian church to officially endorse contraception. Two previous Lambeth Conferences (held in 1908 and 1920) had condemned contraception. But in 1930, by a vote of 193 to 67, the Anglican bishops gave their approval to the birth control movement. As the wording of the *Declaration* indicates, the approval was given with qualification, and almost begrudgingly. But it was given.

Where there is a clearly felt moral obligation to limit or avoid parenthood, the method must be decided by Christian principles. The primary and obvious method is complete abstinence from intercourse (as far as may be necessary) in a life of Christian discipline and self-control in the power of the Holy Spirit. Nevertheless, in those cases where there is such a clearly felt moral obligation to limit or avoid parenthood, and where there is a morally sound reason for avoiding complete abstinence, the Conference agrees that other methods may be used, provided that this is done in the light of the same Christian principles. The Conference records its strong condemnation of any methods of conception-control from motives of selfishness, luxury or mere convenience.[7]

The Lambeth Declaration brought swift reaction from the Roman Catholic hierarchy in England. Cardinal Francis Bourne, the Archbishop of Westminster, deplored "this destructive resolution." "I know," he said in a talk given at Swansea, "the intense surprise and real scandal to the Christian mind which have been caused at home and abroad by this abandonment of the unbroken traditional Christian teaching." In a sharp reprimand directed at the Anglican bishops, he added: "It is recognized that the prelates who adopted this resolution have abdicated any claim which they may have been thought to possess to be authorized exponents of Christian morality."[8]

Cardinal Bourne looked to Rome for support. He found a willing and able ally in the distinguished and influential Jesuit, Arthur Vermeersch, who taught moral theology at the Gregorian University in Rome. Father Vermeersch had his own reasons for wanting the Pope to speak out on the subject of Christian marriage. He was disquieted by various writings emanating from Catholic circles, especially in Germany, that were calling into question certain aspects of the traditional teaching on marriage. He was concerned also, as were other Roman theologians, that there were priests who had become somewhat lax in the confessional in enforcing the Church's ban on contraception.

CASTI CONNUBII

The time seemed ripe for a comprehensive papal statement on Christian marriage. Such a statement became a reality with the publication, on December 31, 1930, of the encyclical, *Casti Connubii*. The encyclical is a remarkable summary of the values of marriage that Christian tradition has defended through the centuries. The discussion of birth control, to which eight paragraphs are devoted, is found in Part Four of the encyclical which speaks of various sins against Christian marriage. Referring to those who call offspring "the disagreeable burden of matrimony," and who sanction the avoidance of this "burden" by the frustration of the marriage act, the encyclical states:

No reason, however grave, can be put forward by which anything intrinsically against nature may become conformable to nature and morally good. Since, therefore, the conjugal act is destined primarily by nature for the begetting of children, those who in exercising it deliberately frustrate its natural power and purpose sin against nature and commit a deed which is shameful and intrinsically vicious.[9]

In obvious reference to the Lambeth Conference which had taken place four months earlier, the encyclical continues: "Some openly departing from the uninterrupted Christian tradition have recently judged it possible solemnly to declare another doctrine regarding this question." This assault against Christian tradition imposes on the Church the duty of reasserting that tradition strongly and without ambiguity:

The Catholic Church, to whom God has entrusted the defense of the integrity and purity of morals, standing erect in the midst of the moral

ruin which surrounds her, that so she may preserve the chastity of the
nuptial union from being defiled by this foul stain, raises her voice in
token of her divine ambassadorship and through Our mouth proclaims
anew: any use whatsoever of matrimony exercised in such a way that the
act is deliberately frustrated in its natural power to generate life is an
offense against the law of God and of nature, and those who indulge in
such are branded with the guilt of a grave sin.[10]

Pastors and others who have the care of souls are warned:

We admonish, therefore, priests who hear confessions and others who have
the care of souls, in virtue of our supreme authority and in our solicitude
for the salvation of souls, not to allow the faithful entrusted to them to err
regarding this most grave law of God; much more that they keep themselves immune from such false opinions, in no way conniving in them. If
any confessor or pastor of souls, which may God forbid, lead the faithful
entrusted to him into these errors or should at least confirm them by
approval or guilty silence, let him be mindful of the fact that he must
render a strict account to God, the Supreme Judge, for the betrayal of his
sacred trust.[11]

In the years following 1930 the various Protestant churches followed
the lead of Lambeth rather than that of Rome. In 1931 the Presbyterian churches in the United States approved the use of contraceptive
methods of birth control. In that same year the Federal Council of
Churches of Christ in America, with a membership of some twenty-
three million, passed the resolution that "the interests of morality and
sound scientific knowledge and the protection of both parents and
children require the repeal of both federal and state laws which prohibit the communication of information about birth control by physicians and other qualified persons."[12]

Over the next three decades a large number of other Protestant
churches gave their endorsement to birth control. They included: the
Church of Sweden, the Presbyterian Church of Ireland, the Calvinist
Church of Holland, the United Lutheran Church of America, the
Methodist Church of the United States of America, the Reformed

Church of France, the Lutheran Church of Finland, the Baptist Union of Denmark.[13]

From 1930 on, then, the lines between Roman Catholics and most other Christians became more and more clearly drawn.

NOTES

1. The word "comstockery," coined by Bernard Shaw, has passed into the English language as a synonym for all forms of violent and repressive censorship.

2. See Heywood Broun and Margaret Leech, *Anthony Comstock, Roundsman of the Lord* (New York: A. & C. Boni, 1927).

3. For a summary of the federal law, see Mary Ware Dennett, *Birth Control Laws* (New York: Hitchcock, 1927), pp. 7–8

4. Robert W. Haney, *Comstockery in America* (Boston: Beacon Press, 1960), p. 20.

5. Broun and Leech, *op. cit.*, p. 16.

6. Lawrence Lader, *The Margaret Sanger Story* (New York: Doubleday & Co., Inc., 1955), p. 97.

7. *Lambeth Conference*, 1930, Declaration 15.

8. Reginald J. Dingle, *Cardinal Bourne at Westminster* (London: Burns & Oates, 1934), p. 165.

9. Pius XI, *Casti Connubii*, par. 55. (All selections from *Casti Connubii* used in this book are taken from *Social Wellsprings*, Vol. 2, (Milwaukee: Bruce Publishing Co., 1942).)

10. *Op. cit.*, par. 57.

11. *Op. cit.*, par. 58.

12. Lader, *op. cit.*, p. 266.

13. Garrett Hardin, ed., *Population, Evolution, and Birth Control* (San Francisco: W. H. Freeman and Co., 1964), p. 224.

II PERSONALIST VALUES IN MARRIAGE

On June 23, 1964, Pope Paul VI spoke to a group of twenty-seven cardinals in his private library. It was the eve of the feast of St. John the Baptist, and the Pope was responding to the felicitations the cardinals had extended to him on his name day. In the course of his remarks, he spoke of "the problem of birth control," which, he said, "everyone is talking about." He described it as "an extremely serious problem," because it touches the source of human life, and the feelings and interests that are closest to the experience of man and woman. At the same time, he pointed out, it is "an extremely complex and delicate question," which involves many spheres of competence, "the most important of which is that of husband and wife, their liberty, their conscience, their love, their duty."

The Church also, he went on to say, has her own competence in this matter, "her own aspect, that of God's law which she interprets, teaches, promotes and defends." The Church has the duty to proclaim the law of God, but this she must do "in the light of scientific, social and psychological truths which in these times have undergone new and very ample study and documentation." To do this requires a thorough study of the theoretical and practical aspects of the problem. The Church has undertaken such a study, the Pope informed the cardinals, "with the help of many and distinguished scholars." The group to which the Pope referred was the Pontifical Study Commission on Family, Population and Birth Problems that had been set up originally in the spring of 1963 by Pope John XXIII and whose membership had recently been increased by Pope Paul himself.

The Pope concluded his remarks on birth control with a word of caution:

But in the meantime, we must say openly that up to now we have not sufficient reason to consider the rules laid down by Pope Pius XII in this matter to be out of date and therefore not binding. These, therefore, must be considered valid, at least so long as we do not feel obliged in conscience to change them. In such a serious matter it seems good that Catholics should want to follow one rule only, that which the Church propounds with authority, and we feel, therefore, that it is opportune to urge that for the moment no one should take it upon himself to make pronouncements differing in terms from the present regulations.[1]

These words of Pope Paul, while not necessarily heralding a change in the Church's teaching on birth control, clearly suggested the presence of uncertainty in the minds of Catholics. The very existence of a papal commission to study the problem of birth control pointed to the ambiguity of the situation. There would be no purpose in setting up such a commission if the Church's position on this problem were unquestionably clear and irrevocably affirmed.

In addition, for the Pope to have said that the rules laid down by his predecessors must be considered valid so long as he does not feel obliged in conscience to change them, suggests at the very least that at the time he spoke the Holy Father was able to contemplate the possibility that at some future time he might feel obliged to change them. The publication, on July 29, 1968, of *Humanae Vitae* makes it clear that four years after making these remarks to the cardinals, the Pope came to the conclusion that he was not obliged in conscience to change the teachings of his predecessors, but, on the contrary, was obliged to reaffirm them.

The question, nonetheless, may rightfully be asked: what happened in the Roman Catholic Church between 1930 and 1964 to create the ambiguities and uncertainties to which the Pope alluded and which took him four years to resolve in his own conscience? What happened during the course of those thirty-four years that brought about the reopening of a question that seemed to have been decisively settled by the encyclical *Casti Connubii?*

This question, however one frames it, is important; it needs to be answered because it is only in the light of the answer that it is possible to understand the reactions that followed the publication of *Humanae Vitae.*

There is no simple and, perhaps, no single answer to the question. One might say that the birth control issue came to the surface of Catholic conscience not so much of its own accord but in the wake of an evolving theology of marriage.

Clearly, one's attitude toward birth control is determined more by one's theology of marriage than by anything intrinsic to that theology. A theology of marriage must be built on values, not on negations. If a person condemns contraception, abortion or divorce, it is not because these condemnations constitute his theology of marriage, but rather because they seem best calculated to protect the positive values which that theology embodies.

Thus the protective norms or rules that one lays down depend upon the values one sees in marriage. A change in the understanding of values could conceivably, though not necessarily, require a change in norms. A deeper understanding of certain values, a shift in priorities of values or a rediscovery of neglected values would, at the very least, force one to take a second look at norms and rules that had been set up in the past as safeguards, and such a reexamination might lead to one of several conclusions: (1) that the norms of the past continue to be adequate and are therefore to be reaffirmed; (2) that the norms of the past are no longer sufficiently adequate to protect the whole complex of marital values and therefore need to be supplemented by other norms, or (3) that the norms of the past actually threaten the values of marriage, as they have come to be understood in a new context, and therefore should be changed.

During the years between 1930 and 1964 there was much discussion in the Roman Catholic Church on the theology of marriage. As a result, many Catholics eventually arrived, with varying degrees of certitude, at the second or third conclusion mentioned in the foregoing paragraph. This fact, it would seem, accounts for the uncertainties and ambiguities to which Pope Paul had alluded. It can be said, then, that one of the reasons for the reopening of the birth control debate in the Catholic Church was the growth and development of the theology of marriage that took place in the years subsequent to the publication of *Casti Connubii*.

THE CONTRIBUTION OF THE LAITY

An important contribution to the renewal of the Church's theology of marriage came, appropriately, from lay organizations devoted to the apostolate of the family. Three such organizations—the Family Renewal Association, the Cana Conference Movement, and the Catholic Family Movement—are especially deserving of mention. Originating in the United States, these groups represented a distinctively American contribution to the life and thought of the Church.

The Family Renewal Association came into being in the early 1940's, largely through the efforts of an energetic Jesuit priest in New York City, John P. Delaney, associate editor of *America*. Its principal achievement was the organization, in New York City and elsewhere, of biannual "family renewal days." These "days," centering around the celebration of the Eucharist, involved conferences and dialogue. The conferences, in which such topics as the vocation of marriage, the mutual love of husband and wife, and the meaning of sexuality in marriage were discussed, proved to be for many couples a refreshingly different approach to marriage—an approach that emphasized the personal values of the marriage relationship rather than its juridical elements. The dialogue during these renewal days brought about a sharing by married couples of their experiences in living these personal values.

The Family Renewal Movement left a deep impression on those

who became involved, but it never became a widespread or well-known movement. When Father Delaney was transferred to the Philippines, the ideas that he had initiated were absorbed to a large extent by the Cana Conference Movement. In the beginning, at least, the Cana Conference represented fundamentally the same approach as Family Renewal, with perhaps a stronger orientation toward discussions of very practical matters involved in the husband-wife, parent-children relationships.

The many apostolic-minded Catholics drawn to Cana, often from the ranks of Young Christian Student (Y.C.S.) groups, helped to bring into being yet another organization concerned with the family apostolate—the Christian Family Movement (C.F.M.). From its beginnings the Christian Family Movement was an action group that visualized its apostolate as reaching beyond itself to the environment in which its members sought to bear witness to the values involved in Christian marriage and family life.

These lay organizations—Family Renewal, Cana, C.F.M.—introduced a new phenomenon into the life of the Church in America: a generation of young married couples who were reflecting theologically on the meaning of their life together. They saw marriage as a vocation to which God had called them, in which their love for one another and their expression of this love through intercourse were not obstacles to or mere adjuncts of sanctity, but the instrument and means of achieving it. They became increasingly aware that marriage was much more than a juridical contract in which certain rights relating to the generation of offspring were given and received; it was a community of love resulting from the gift of one's self to the other, a gift which, by enabling each to participate in the life of the other, brought personal enrichment and Christian fulfillment to both. Marital intercourse was seen as being at once a symbol and an effective cause of this community of love; consequently it had a significance that could not be expressed simply in terms of its procreative purpose. In the context of this growing appreciation of the personal values of married life and married love, it seemed increasingly unrealistic to think that the nature of marriage could be adequately expressed in the impersonal categories of primary and secondary purposes—a view that had for so long a time dominated the theological approach to marriage.

THE CONTRIBUTION OF CATHOLIC SCHOLARS

These new insights of married couples reflected the views of certain philosophers and theologians who were attempting to develop an approach to marriage which, while preserving continuity with the tradition of the past, would open itself to contemporary understandings of the meaning of married life. A pioneer in this attempt was Dietrich von Hildebrand, professor of philosophy at the University of Munich, "the first layman to make a substantial contribution to the Catholic doctrine on marriage."[2]

In 1925 von Hildebrand gave a series of lectures to university students at Innsbruck on the nature of purity and virginity. These lectures were expanded into a book, published in German in 1927, which was translated into English in 1930 under the title *In Defense of Purity*. The book attempted to show how sexuality, married love and procreation are related.

Von Hildebrand affirmed that of all the activities and appetites of man rooted in his bodily nature, sex occupies a unique place. In explaining the uniqueness of human sexuality, he explicitly rejected the analogy, common in Christian tradition since Augustine, which likened intercourse to other bodily appetites, such as the appetite for food. Other bodily experiences, von Hildebrand maintained, were characterized by lack of depth. "Delight in a good dinner, for example, or annoyance at a bad one, belongs of its nature to the superficial zone of human experience."[3] Sexual experiences, on the other hand, "display a depth and gravity which remove them altogether from the province of other bodily experiences."[4] They produce an effect which transcends the physical sphere and incorporates them into experiences of a higher order that are psychological and spiritual.

The reason for the uniqueness of human sexuality is its relationship to love, specifically to wedded love. Other bodily experiences find their sole significance in terms of their end or object. Thus the significance of eating consists precisely in the achievement of its objective purpose, the maintenance of life. "The act of wedded communion," on the contrary, "has indeed the object of procreation, but in addition the *significance* of a unique union of love."[5] Married sexuality, in other words, does not have only one function, namely, the generation of offspring. It also has, apart from that function, another and deep-rooted meaning for man as a human being; it is the expression of the wedded love of man and woman, and a fulfillment of their personal longing for communion with one another.

To overlook the union between physical sex and love or its significance and to recognize only the purely utilitarian bond between sex and the propagation of the race is to degrade man and to be blind to the meaning of this mysterious domain.[6]

Von Hildebrand's special contribution to the theology of marriage was this insistence that the act of sexual intercourse has an *intrinsic significance* for husband and wife that cannot be identified with or reduced to nothing more than the fulfillment of its *objective end*. Procreation is not simply the achievement of a biological finality in intercourse; it is, at a much deeper level, the fruit of the mystery of that wedded love toward which intercourse is ordered by its intrinsic nature.

In his later writings von Hildebrand expressed his understanding of the uniqueness of human sexuality in terms of what he called the principle of superabundance, which he distinguished from the principle of instrumental finality. In the case of instrumental finality, the value of an instrument is identified with its purpose. A knife, for example, is an instrument for cutting; its value as a knife is fulfilled in its being able to cut. In superabundant finality, however, that which is a *means* to something also has a value in itself. The act of intercourse has as its meaning and value the unique love-fulfillment that flows from the mutual self-giving of husband and wife. "But to this high good that has a meaning and value in itself has been entrusted procreation."[7] The same act which in its meaning is constitutive of the closest love union has been superabundantly made the source of procreation. Thus, while procreation may be spoken of as an end, it is not mere instrumental causality; it is, rather, an instance of the finality of superabundance.

The ideas of von Hildebrand were taken up and expanded by a German priest, Herbert Doms. His influential book, *The Meaning of Marriage,* appeared in Germany in 1935, just five years after the publication of *Casti Connubii*. The English translation of his work was published in 1939. Doms was trained in biology and psychology before he became a priest. This training, combined with his theological studies, made him particularly qualified to contribute to a rethinking of the Church's doctrine on marriage.

In the introduction to his book Doms pointed out that the understanding of marriage developed by von Hildebrand was not so novel as some might have thought; that actually this emphasis on marriage as a community rather than as merely an institution for the reproduction and education of children had for many centuries been a part of the tradition of the Catholic Church. There had been, Doms said, two schools of thought in that tradition: the one saw the child as the principal purpose of marriage; the other emphasized more the unity of husband and wife, and the help they give one another in achieving perfection. With an impressive list of citations from this latter stream of thought (including St. Bonaventure, the *Catechism* of the Council of Trent, St. Alphonsus Liguori, and a number of nineteenth century theologians) the author pointed out that it was by no means foreign to Catholic tradition to admit that marriage has another essential purpose besides procreation, namely, community of personal life between husband and wife.

Aligning himself with this position, Doms maintained that the unity realized by the act of intercourse is not simply or even principally unity on the physical level; it is, in a mysterious but very real sense, a unity that is metaphysical, i.e., beyond the physical. It involves a transformation that leaves a deep imprint on the personalities of both husband and wife. The gift that they make to one another is not simply the gift of their sexual organs but of their whole persons, for a man and woman are ordinarily drawn to one another, and eventually to marriage and marital union, not primarily by the desire to have children but by the desire to achieve personal fulfillment from their two-in-oneness. Even in the exceptional case, where the desire for the child is from the beginning as strong as the love for the partner, that desire is eminently directed to personal fulfillment. The woman says, "I want to be a mother." She does not say, "The species must continue," or "It is my duty to have a child."[8]

It is therefore a violation of the personal dignity of both partners to ignore this aspect of personal transformation in marriage for the sake of "something apart" from it, whether that "something apart" be the child or even the subjective satisfaction which intercourse affords.

In other words, the immanent meaning of the union of two persons in marriage "does not consist in their subservience to a purpose outside themselves *for* which they marry,"[9] nor even in their giving of mutual help. Instead, marital union, which has its own meaning and its own distinctive metaphysical characteristics, is a deep and real thing in itself, quite apart from the fact that it also exists for something outside itself, whether that something is described as its primary purpose (procreation) or its secondary purpose (mutual help). In Doms' view—and in this he anticipated the teaching of Vatican II—we will arrive at a better understanding of marriage if we abandon the classical terminology that speaks of marriage in terms of "primary" and "secondary" purposes. "It would be better," he wrote, "if we just spoke of the procreative and personal purposes immanent in marriage and distinguished them from its meaning."[10]

Though the summary in the preceding paragraphs is brief, it is sufficient to show that there was in the Roman Catholic community a growing recognition of the personalist dimensions of marriage, and a concomitant desire to develop a theology that would do greater justice to these dimensions than had been done by marriage manuals in the past. There was, in short, an awakening realization that theology, if it was to deal realistically with marriage, could not be content to draw conclusions from merely an abstract understanding of the subject; it must also take into account the light shed on the meaning of the marriage experience by men and women actually living it.

This is not to say that these new developments in the theological understanding of marriage immediately opened the way to a more sympathetic approach toward birth control. On the contrary, both von Hildebrand and Doms unequivocally condemned any deliberate human intervention in intercourse, nor did they see any conflict between such condemnation and the personalist view of marriage that they proposed. To distinguish the meaning of the sexual act from its procreative purpose was one thing, but to separate the act itself from that purpose by deliberate human intervention was quite another. The latter was always morally wrong, because control of the biological finality of intercourse rested solely with God. As Doms said:

In our opinion artificial intervention in the procreative process is evil, not so much because living matter is wasted or because another person's right to existence is violated, as because of the voluntary attack on vital processes in which we have no right to interfere. The sin is not that against a human person who does not yet exist, but against the sovereign rights of God himself.[11]

Von Hildebrand wrote in a similar vein:

The sinfulness of artificial birth control is rooted in the fact that one arrogates to oneself the right to separate the actualized love union in marriage from a possible procreation, to sever this wonderful, deeply mysterious connection, instituted by God, approaching this mystery in an irreverent attitude. We are here confronted with the basic sin of irreverence toward God, the denial of our creaturehood, the acting as if we were our own lords.[12]

Married couples involved in the various family movements previously mentioned reached very much the same conclusion. Their increased awareness of the Christian dignity of their married vocation brought with it a corresponding appreciation of the dignity of Christian parenthood. Having children was an important part of the personal fulfillment that they saw as the meaning of marriage. Parenthood meant responding not to a biological necessity, but to the will of God as He spoke to man and woman through the concrete circumstances of their married lives. One of the distinctive elements in the spirituality of marriage that developed in the 1940's and early 1950's was an emphasis on the importance of a generous openness to life. Parents were urged to accept children as God sent them and to rely on divine Providence for help in caring for them. This was the theme of a number of books that appeared about this time. One, edited by Maisie Ward, bears the significant title *Be Not Solicitous*. It presents a series of human interest stories that show "a multitude of lives all lovingly and personally guided by God, sometimes through sorrow, sometimes through joy."[13] The theme of the book is, in the editor's words, "God's Providence in relation to Catholic families who put their trust in him."[14]

NOTES

1. Paul VI, *Acta Apostolicae Sedis,* July 31, 1964. (All selections from *Acta Apostolicae Sedis* used in this book are from the N.C. News Service translation.)

2. John T. Noonan, *Contraception: A History of its Treatment by the Catholic Theologians and Canonists* (Cambridge, Mass., Harvard University Press, 1965), p. 495.

3. Dietrich von Hildebrand, *In Defense of Purity* (New York: Sheed and Ward, Inc., 1935), p. 11.

4. *Op. cit.,* p. 13.

5. *Op. cit.,* p. 22.

6. *Op. cit.,* p. 24.

7. Dietrich von Hildebrand, "Marriage and Overpopulation," *Thought* 36 (1961), p. 93.

8. Herbert Doms, *The Meaning of Marriage* (New York: Sheed and Ward, Inc., 1939), pp. 37–38.

9. *Op. cit.,* p. 87.

10. *Op. cit.,* p. 88.

11. *Op. cit.,* p. 73.

12. Von Hildebrand, "Marriage and Overpopulation," p. 96.

13. Maisie Ward, *Be Not Solicitous* (New York: Sheed and Ward, Inc., 1953), p. 42.

14. *Ibid.*

III THE DEBATE
ON RHYTHM

The emphasis in the forties and fifties on a generous openness to life does not mean that there was no awareness of both the psychological and economic problems that could be created in particular situations by a large family. It does not mean, either, that there were no efforts made in the Catholic community to find a workable solution for these problems. A topic frequently discussed in Catholic circles during this time (and even earlier) was the so-called "safe period," or the rhythm method of family limitation.

It had long been known that there are certain times in the month when a woman is less likely to conceive, but the physiological reasons for this fact remained obscure. The year 1930 saw the publication of the results of two research projects on the "safe period." These investigations, conducted independently by a Japanese gynecologist, Dr. K. Ogino, and Professor H. Knaus of the University of Prague, provided a scientific basis for understanding and estimating the rhythm of fertility and infertility in a woman's cycle. The discoveries of Ogino and Knaus were popularized by an American gynecologist, Leo J. Latz, in a book titled *The Rhythm of Sterility and Fertility in Women*. The fact that between 1932 and 1944 the book went through seventeen printings and sold more than 200,000 copies is ample evidence that there was widespread interest in the subject that it discussed.

Yet rhythm did not become what some people wanted to call it—

"the Catholic method of birth control." To many, openness to parent-hood and reliance on divine Providence still remained the Catholic ideal. Recourse to the practice of rhythm was looked upon, initially at least, as an emergency measure to solve "hard cases." In the moral theology courses at Catholic seminaries, future priests were warned that they must not take the initiative in recommending the use of rhythm, though they might suggest it cautiously in those cases where spouses could not otherwise be deterred from practicing other forms of birth control. In 1946 Gerald Kelly, Jesuit professor of moral theology at St. Mary's College, St. Marys, Kansas, summarized the thinking of many Catholic moralists when he wrote in *Theological Studies:* "Only exceptional couples can take up the practice of the "rhythm-theory" without exposing their married lives to grave dangers; and even these couples usually need the special grace of God."[1]

SOCIAL CHANGES

The years following World War II produced many sociological changes that were to have profound influences on the family. The attraction of urban living brought more and more people to the cities, where residential accommodations were often crowded and restricted. Competition for advancement in a highly technological society made higher education an increasingly practical necessity for the young. As a result, parents—many of whom had considered themselves for-tunate to have completed high school—found themselves faced with the heavy financial burden of sending their children to college and even to graduate school.

The problems created by these sociological changes gave rise to questions in the Roman Catholic community which an earlier gen-eration would have thought impertinent or, indeed, un-Christian. Did not the actual circumstances under which all but the very wealthy families lived suggest the practical necessity for some form of birth limitation? Was it any longer realistic to propose, for most families at least, the ideal of "generous" parenthood? Did not the responsibility toward existing children and their total education take precedence over the responsibility to generate more children?

THE PASTORAL PROBLEM

New questions invariably force a reexamination of established positions. Theologians began to reappraise the grudging approval they had heretofore given to the practice of rhythm. The problem for the theologian was not the theoretical question of whether the practice of rhythm under certain circumstances was justifiable in marriage; this question had long since been answered, however reluctantly, in the affirmative. The problem now calling for more serious discussion was the practical one of determining what circumstances would justify the practice of rhythm. Were they many or few? Could rhythm be recommended to Catholic parents as a normal element of family planning or as an emergency measure in extraordinary cases? Was it a positive Christian way of cooperating in God's plan, or did its use under any circumstances imply a lack of trust in divine Providence?

There was no consistent pastoral approach to these questions in the two decades following 1930. Pastors and confessors inclined more or less toward two theological opinions, both acknowledging the licitness of rhythm but each justifying it from a totally different perspective. The more rigorist opinion maintained that the practice of rhythm was *per se* illicit and only *per accidens* licit.[2] In other words, it was illicit in itself, since marriage, of its essence, must be ordered to procreation; it could, however, become licit in those circumstances where there were reasons serious enough to warrant its use.

The more lenient opinion was that the practice of rhythm was *per se* licit because, while the human race in general obviously bears the responsibility to procreate, there was no basis for believing that the duty to do so should be imposed on any particular couple. On the other hand, if a couple's reason for practicing rhythm was founded solely on a selfish unwillingness to accept the responsibilities of married life, rhythm would then be, *per accidens,* illicit.[3]

This inconsistency in the pastoral approach produced an unhealthy state of confusion. The answer to whether rhythm was justified in a particular case seemed to be dependent on finding the "right" confessor. Moreover, the situation was further confused by the fact that many pastors and confessors continued to be cautious about communicating any information whatsoever on the subject. Even "sympathetic" confessors were often reluctant to take the initiative in recommending the practice.

POPE PIUS XII AND THE
ALLOCUTIONS OF 1951

Reflection on the proper pastoral approach to the use of rhythm was given a new direction by Pope Pius XII in two allocutions which he delivered in 1951. The first was addressed to the Italian Catholic Society of Midwives on October 29. The most complete papal statement on marriage since *Casti Connubii,* it discussed the morality of rhythm in some detail. The Pope referred to "the serious question today as to whether and how far the obligation of ready disposition to serve motherhood can be reconciled with the ever more widely diffused recourse to the periods of natural sterility."[4]

The members of the society were urged to be well-informed on the medical aspects of rhythm, since it was their responsibility, rather than the priest's, to instruct married people about the biological and technical facts of the theory. Nor was it sufficient merely to be familiar with the pertinent scientific data; they must also be prepared to clarify the moral principles involved. The licit use of rhythm, the Pontiff said, depended on whether or not the intention to restrict intercourse to sterile periods was based on adequate moral grounds. He went on to explain that there were serious motives, "not rarely present," of a medical, eugenic, economic, and social nature that could exempt spouses "for a long time, even for the entire duration of marriage" from the positive obligation of having children. Consequently, he concluded, "the observance of the sterile periods can be licit on moral grounds," and "actually is so"[5] when the serious motives are present.

This statement of Pope Pius XII on the morality of rhythm had broad pastoral implications. Rhythm, providing there were justifiable reasons for its use, was open to all Christian couples. It was not to be regarded merely as an emergency measure to meet extraordinary situations. There was no attempt, either, on the part of the Pope to present rhythm simply as a deterrent to onanism—an approach that had been so common in the moral theology manuals. On the contrary, the Pope seemed to suggest that "the ever widely diffused recourse to the periods of natural sterility" was quite understandable and acceptable, since valid reasons for the use of rhythm were by no means rare.

Lest there be any doubt about the pastoral concern that had motivated his remarks to the midwives, the Pope, in another allocution a month later—on November 26, 1951—made clear his desire "to consider with sympathy and understanding the real difficulties of the married state in our day."[6] This allocution was given, significantly, to the National Congress of the Family Front and the Association of Large Families. Referring to his October statement, the Pope said: "In our last allocution on conjugal morality we affirmed the legitimacy and, at the same time, the limits—in truth very broad—of a regulation of offspring which, unlike so-called birth control, is compatible with the law of God."[7]

The use by a Pope for the first time of the term "regulation of offspring" was a significant addition to the official Roman Catholic vocabulary on marriage. It pointed the way from an exclusive emphasis on the ideal of "generous" parenthood to an important complementary emphasis on "responsible" parenthood. The allocution therefore set at rest the anxiety of many Catholic parents—that the use of rhythm, even when circumstances seemed clearly to call for it, expressed a less than total commitment to their vocation.

A NEW PRINCIPLE?

The meaning of a statement at the time it is uttered is not always the same as the meaning it assumes in the light of later reflection. There were two ways of understanding the judgment made by Pope Pius XII on the morality of rhythm. The first was to see it within the framework of traditional Catholic moral principles. According to these principles, the morality of an action depends on (1) the object (i.e., the act considered in itself), (2) the intention of the agent, and (3) the moral circumstances in which the act is performed. Rhythm, according to the Pope's statement, was justifiable when there were serious reasons for its use because, unlike artificial methods of birth control, it did not violate the nature of the act of intercourse. This meant that rhythm was in itself morally indifferent. It became good, therefore, if the intention underlying its use was good (i.e., if the serious reasons required were actually present), and if the circumstances were good (i.e., if both spouses agreed to its use and the abstinence which rhythm necessitated did not involve the danger of incontinence or infidelity). This was the interpretation placed on the Pope's words by most theologians at the time and this was the way that the moral theology manuals, following the direction of the papal statement, began to present the morality of rhythm.

The second possible interpretation was that the Pope's statement actually introduced a new principle into the Church's moral teaching on marriage, namely, that in the instance of rhythm, at least, it was permissible to separate sexual intercourse from its procreative purpose. Some theologians, while conceding that the papal statement admitted of such an interpretation, nevertheless would not agree that it was the one the Pope intended. Their point was that approval of rhythm would imply the approval of deliberate efforts to use scientific knowledge to avoid pregnancy; this, in turn, would seem to sanction the use of scientific knowledge to separate the act of intercourse—at least as far as rhythm was concerned—from its ordination to procreation.

Gregory Baum, O.S.A., interpreted the papal statement in this way:

Before (the papal statement) Catholic theologians had regarded the sexual act in married life to be justified and holy by its ordination to procreation. They had permitted married couples to have sexual intercourse even when they could not hope to have any children. But they did not conceive of any sexual activity in married life carried on with the positive intention of excluding conception. This was regarded as unnatural, against the very nature of the sexual act, and hence gravely sinful.

When the Catholic Church officially approved the rhythm method, it acknowledged for the first time that sexuality in marriage was a value as such. Sexual love could be meaningful, good and holy without being directly related to the generation of a child. By permitting the rhythm method, the Catholic Church taught that it was licit and sometimes of obligation for Christian couples to seek the joy and mutual encouragement in sexual union while not desiring another child. This was new.[8]

This interpretation, if acceptable, obviously meant that the implications in the papal statement went considerably beyond the teaching proposed by von Hildebrand and Doms. It was also evident that if such a principle were established as part of the Church's teaching on marriage, the door would eventually be opened to discussions of methods other than rhythm for birth limitation. Inevitably, then, the question would have to be faced: why is the separation of intercourse and the ordination to procreation permissible only in the case of rhythm?

NOTES

1. Gerald Kelly, "Notes on Moral Theology," *Theological Studies* 7 (1946), pp. 105–106.

2. See Orville N. Griese, *The Morality of Periodic Continence* (Washington, D.C.: Catholic University Press, 1943).

3. Hugh O'Connell, "Is Rhythm per se Illicit?" *American Ecclesiastical Review* 119 (November, 1948), pp. 336–347.

4. Pius XII, "Apostolate of the Midwife," *Catholic Mind* (January, 1952), p. 56.

5. *Op. cit.,* p. 57.

6. Pius XII, "Morality in Marriage," *Catholic Mind* (May, 1952), p. 311.

7. *Ibid.*

8. Thomas D. Roberts, ed., *Contraception and Holiness* (New York: Herder & Herder, Inc., 1964), p. 337.

IV THE FIRST PHASE
OF THE DEBATE
ON THE PILL

As we have seen in the preceding chapter, a number of factors during the 1950's made it clear that the discussion of birth regulation among Catholics could no longer be confined only to rhythm. The possibility of a broader interpretation of the papal allocutions of 1951 was one of these factors. Another factor—and perhaps a more important one—was the scientific development of sterilizing drugs or, as they are better known, contraceptive pills.

The lively discussion set off by the advent of the contraceptive pill can be divided into two phases. The first phase extended roughly from 1953 to 1963. During this time Catholic moralists worked for the most part within the framework of the traditional Catholic condemnation of all forms of contraceptive intercourse and debated on the possible circumstances in which the pill could be used without falling under that condemnation. The second phase, beginning in 1963, amounted to a reopening in the Catholic ethical world of the issue of contraception itself—an issue that seemingly had been closed by *Casti Connubii* in 1930. Some theologians began to question (cautiously at first, more openly as time went on) the traditional presentation of natural law doctrine that had been used by Catholic moralists as the basis for condemning contraception.[1] The debate moved gradually from the question, What are the circumstances in which the use of the pill would not be considered directly contraceptive and would therefore be permissible? to the broader question, Are there circumstances in which the use of the pill, even when directly contraceptive, might be justified? It is this continuing debate that has divided the Catholic theological world and this division that has brought such strong reactions to Pope Paul's encyclical reaffirming the traditional condemnation of contraception.

THE CONTRACEPTIVE PILL

The first contraceptive pill to appear on the commercial market was the sterilizing drug called phosphorylated hesperidin, developed by Dr. Benjamin Sieve of Boston. In October, 1952, Dr. Sieve published a report on the success of his experiment in which hesperidin was used to produce temporary sterility in three hundred married couples.[2] This pill, taken orally by both husband and wife for a prescribed period of time, was supposed to render the ovum impenetrable by the male sperm. The temporary sterility thus induced disappeared shortly after use of the pill was discontinued.

Catholic moralists who commented on the use of hesperidin were unanimous in their moral appraisal. Using the drug amounted to contraceptive sterilization; having intercourse during the drug-induced sterile period was contraceptive intercourse. On both scores, therefore, the use of hesperidin was declared morally illicit. In two articles in the *Linacre Quarterly*, John J. Lynch, S.J., professor of moral theology at Weston College, Weston, Massachusetts, presented his evaluation of the morality of hesperidin. His first article[3] concluded that the initial and essential malice of fertility control through the use of hesperidin derived from its violation of the Fifth Commandment, since it was a form of self-mutilation known as direct sterilization. In his second article[4] he noted that those who made use of marriage, after they had by their own volition deprived themselves of the power to procreate, incurred the additional malice of a sin against the Sixth Commandment for, by intent, and in effect, their act of intercourse was contraceptive, onanistic, illicit birth prevention.[5]

The morality of the use of hesperidin is today largely a matter of academic interest. Apparently it did not live up to the expectations of those who developed it. It was never widely used and, though some experimentation with it continues, it seems no longer to be recommended.

PROGESTERONE PILLS

The oral contraceptives that are now in use and that have become the subject of so much debate are the synthetic progesterone pills. Developed in 1953 and tested extensively in Puerto Rico in 1956, they were approved for commercial sale in the United States in 1960. The progesterone pill makes conception impossible by duplicating artificially in a non-pregnant woman, a process that occurs naturally during pregnancy.

When a woman is pregnant nature produces the hormone progesterone, which prevents ovulation. The contraceptive pill, containing as it does a synthetic progesterone compound, produces the same effect. (For this reason, the progesterone pills are often referred to as anovulants.) Since this suppression of ovulation effects a temporary sterilization, the pills are contraceptive agents precisely because they are sterilizing agents.

If temporary sterilization and the consequent prevention of conception were the only effects of the pill, Catholic moralists would have found it relatively simple to make the judgment that use of the pill was morally wrong because direct sterilization and contraceptive intercourse were morally wrong. What complicated the moral evaluation of the pill was the fact that it can also be used to produce other effects that are good and desirable and, according to the traditional principle of the double effect, an action that has multiple effects and is not evil in itself is permissible if (1) the good effect follows directly from the action, (2) the agent intends only the good effect, and (3) the good effect intended is proportionate to the evil effect permitted. When these conditions are fulfilled, the evil effect may be permitted for the sake of the greater good.

With this principle of the double effect in mind, Catholic moralists discussed the morality of the pill. Medical evidence indicated that the pill could be therapeutic as well as contraceptive, i.e., in addition to its sterilizing and contraceptive effects, it could remedy certain pathological conditions. In view of these therapeutic benefits, the temporary sterilization resulting from the pill, with the concomitant prevention of conception, could be permitted where conditions for the principle of the double effect were verified.

PIUS XII AND THE PILL

The basic soundness of this distinction between the sterilizing effect of the pill and the therapeutic benefits it could produce was confirmed by Pope Pius XII in his address to the Seventh International Congress of Hematology on September 12, 1958. Speaking to the question of the morality of the pill, a question which he said was "often discussed today among doctors and moralists," the Pope stated:

The answer depends on the intention of the person. If a woman takes such medicine, not to prevent conception, but only on the advice of a doctor as a necessary remedy because of the condition of the uterus or the organism, she produces *indirect* sterilization, which is permitted according to the general principles governing acts with a double effect. But a *direct* and, therefore illicit sterilization results when ovulation is stopped to protect the uterus and the organism from the consequences of a pregnancy which it is not able to sustain. Some moralists contend that it is permissible to take medicines with this latter intention, but they are in error.

It is likewise necessary to reject the view of a number of doctors and moralists who permit these practices when medical indications make conception undesirable, or in other similar cases, which cannot be discussed here. In these cases the use of medication has as its end the prevention of conception by preventing ovulation. They are instances, therefore, of direct sterilization.[6]

THERAPEUTIC USES OF THE PILL

In the continuing discussion on the pill that followed the papal statement, moral theologians set about the task of determining which uses
of the pill served a genuine therapeutic purpose and therefore could
be justified in accordance with traditional principles. The following
uses for the pill were discussed:

1. *Correction of menstrual disorders.* There was unanimous agreement among the moral theologians that it was morally permissible
to use the progesterone pill for the correction of various menstrual
disorders (e.g., excessive or prolonged menstruation or abnormal
menstrual bleeding).[7]

2. *Regulation of the ovulatory cycle.* Moralists in general agreed
that the use of the pill was justifiable to correct an irregular menstrual cycle. In the discussion of this problem much debate centered
around the precise meaning of "irregularity." Since there is no such
thing as a completely regular cycle, a determination had to be made
on what degree of irregularity would constitute a pathological condition that the pill could be used to correct. The most rigorist position was that taken by Lawrence L. McReavy, professor of moral
theology at Ushaw College, Durham, England, and a frequent con-
tributor to the English journal *The Clergy Review*. Father McReavy
expressed doubt that gynecologists would consider irregularity, however pronounced, a truly pathological condition. He was inclined,
therefore, to question the licitness of the use of the pill for regulating
the menstrual cycle.[8]

He was almost alone, however, in his stand; other theologians offered more liberal views. Some suggested that any condition of irregularity that would prompt a woman to consult a physician could
be considered pathological.[9] Others suggested—and they represented
the position most commonly accepted—that any degree of irregularity
which would preclude a reasonably effective use of rhythm could be
considered abnormal and therefore, in the wide sense of the term, at

least, pathological. Such a condition would justify the use of the pill.[10] Still more liberal was the view taken by John R. Connery, S.J., who wrote:

Would it be permissible to use the drug in cases where the irregularity was within the normal range but still such as to make the practice of periodic continence difficult? Would it be licit (if it were medically feasible) so to regularize the period that it would always be twenty-eight days and ovulation would always take place on the fourteenth day? I really do not see why it would not. I see no moral reason why one must be limited to what is normal. It seems to me that perfect regularity is as legitimate a goal as perfect health or perfect vision. As long as nothing is done to suppress ovulation in any particular cycle, I do not think the use of drugs to pinpoint the day of ovulation can be considered sterilizing in any real sense. Sterilization does not consist in determining ovulation; it consists in suppressing it. I would feel quite sure that if the drug were used to determine ovulation accurately with a view to actually achieving a pregnancy, no one would object. If it is not wrong in this instance, I do not see why it must be questioned when used to avoid a pregnancy by those who have a legitimate reason to do so.[11]

3. *Suppression of ovulation during lactation.* Far less agreement existed among moralists regarding the use of the pill during the *post partum* period of lactation. The possibility of doing so in this situation was first proposed in 1958 by Canon Louis Janssens, professor of theology at the University of Louvain.[12] Janssens reasoned that since ovulation is normally suspended during the time of lactation, use of the pill would be permissible in order to make certain that nature did not fail to provide this period of natural sterility. The pill, under this circumstance, would not frustrate nature but simply guarantee its normal operation.

Janssens' position could be understood in either of two ways: in this one instance, he was justifying direct sterilization (in which case his opinion would amount to a repudiation of a principle traditionally accepted by theologians and confirmed by Pius XII), or he was, in effect, suggesting a redefinition of direct sterilization that would restrict its meaning to the suppression of the *normal* generative function. Sterilization, thus redefined, would be direct only when it rendered a woman sterile at a time when she should be fertile. Suppression of ovulation at a time when a woman normally should be sterile, therefore, would not be included in the definition of direct sterilization.

Janssens' view received support from the Irish theologian, Dennis O'Callaghan,[13] but the majority of moralists took issue with it. Those who felt that Janssens' opinion tended to justify direct sterilization, simply adverted to the traditional position that direct sterilization is never permissible. They maintained that one may never directly intend his own sterility, for an individual's right over the generative function was limited to its use or non-use, and nothing more.[14] Positive suppression of the reproductive function was therefore not within the domain of the individual.

Others disagreed with Janssens because they saw inherent in his position the possibility of the way being opened for the use of other contraceptives. They argued that if the pill, an artifice created by man, could be used to control fertility, there would be no reason for excluding the use of other such artifices. Joseph J. Farraher, S.J., expressed this criticism in these words: "Anovulants are certainly not an exact replacement of natural substances and are certainly artificial means; so why not other contraceptives in similar circumstances?"[15]

The validity of Janssens' position was also questioned on medical grounds. Was it medically sound to say that ovulation during the time of lactation must be considered abnormal? Was it really nature's intention that this time should be a period of sterility? This would seem difficult to prove. Dr. John R. Cavanagh, a physician and psychiatrist, cited a number of scientific studies which seemed to cast doubt on Janssens' basic presupposition, and concluded that "it seems apparent that Father Janssens arrived at his conclusion more hopefully than factually."[16]

4. *"Ovulation rebound."* It is clear from the foregoing that theologians were divided in the answers they gave to the question, Was

it permissible to suppress ovulation in order to *guarantee sterility* in a woman who was supposed to be naturally sterile? Quite a different problem was posed by the question, was it permissible to suppress ovulation in order to *produce fertility* in a woman who was actually sterile? This was the problem of the so-called "ovulation rebound."

There was some evidence that if the pill was used for several months to suppress ovulation in a sterile woman, fertility often resulted when use of the pill was discontinued. Was such a procedure permissible? The theologians who commented on this problem believed so. They reasoned that the malice of direct sterilization consisted not in the suppression of ovulation, but in the sterility that was caused by it. In the case in question, suppression of ovulation could hardly be said to cause a sterility that already existed. In other words, the suppression of ovulation was not necessarily identical with sterilization. A hysterectomy, for example, would render a woman permanently sterile. If later on this same woman underwent an ovariectomy, the surgery could not in any proper sense of the term be described as a sterilizing operation because it was impossible to sterilize some one who was already sterile. Analogously, in the case of "ovulation rebound," while there was temporary suspension of the ovarian function, it could not be said that this was the cause of sterilization, since sterility was already present.[17]

NOTES

1. See, e.g., Herbert McCabe, "Contraceptives and Natural Law," *New Blackfriars* 46 (November, 1964), pp. 89–96.

2. Benjamin Sieve, "A New Anti-Fertility Factor," *Science* 116 (October 10, 1952), pp. 373–385.

3. John J. Lynch, "Fertility Control and the Moral Law," *Linacre Quarterly* 20 (August, 1953), pp. 83–89.

4. John J. Lynch, "Another Moral Aspect of Fertility Control," *Linacre Quarterly* 20 (November, 1953), pp. 118–122.

5. See André Snoeck, "Fecundation inhibée et morale Catholique," *Nouvelle Revue Theologique* 75 (July-August, 1953), pp. 690–702. Father Snoeck, pro-

fessor at the Jesuit Scholasticate in Louvain, is in substantial agreement with Father Lynch.

6. Pius XII, "Morality and Eugenics," *The Pope Speaks* 6 (December, 1960), p. 395.

7. Francis J. Connell, "Answers to Questions," *American Ecclesiastical Review* 143 (September, 1960), pp. 203–205; John J. Lynch, "Moral Aspects of Pharmaceutical Fertility Control," *Proceedings of the Catholic Theological Society of America* (1958), pp. 127–138.

8. Lawrence L. McReavy, "Use of Steroid Drugs to Regularize Menstrual Cycles," *The Clergy Review* 46 (December, 1961), pp. 746–750.

9. Dennis O'Callaghan, "Fertility Control by Hormonal Medication," *Irish Theological Quarterly* 27 (January, 1960), pp. 1–15.

10. Connell, *op. cit.,* Richard A. McCormick, "Anti-Fertility Pills," *Homiletic and Pastoral Review* 62 (May, 1962), pp. 697–698.

11. John R. Connery, "Notes on Moral Theology," *Theological Studies* 19 (December, 1958), p. 550.

12. Louis Janssens, "L'Inhibition de l'ovulation est-elle moralement licite?" *Ephemerides Theologicae Lovanienses* 34 (April-June, 1958), pp. 357–360.

13. O'Callaghan, *op. cit.,* p. 14.

14. Joseph J. Farraher, "Notes on Moral Theology," *Theological Studies* 22 (December, 1961), p. 628.

15. *Op. cit.,* p. 629.

16. John R. Cavanagh, *The Popes, the Pill and the People* (Milwaukee: Bruce Publishing Co., 1965), p. 80.

17. The fairly abundant literature on the use of the pill focuses for the most part on the four areas discussed above. In somewhat more cursory fashion, the following topics were also discussed:

1. The use of the pill to delay menstruation for more convenient participation in some important events, e.g., an athletic event. See Richard McCormick, "Anti-Fertility Pills," *Homiletic and Pastoral Review* 62 (May, 1962), pp. 699–700.

2. The use of the pill in the case of extreme fear of pregnancy. See John J. Farraher, "Notes on Moral Theology," *Theological Studies* 21 (December, 1960), pp. 601–602.

3. The use of the pill by a woman in danger of rape. See John C. Ford and Gerald Kelly, *Contemporary Moral Theology,* Vol. 2 (Westminster, Md., Newman Press, 1964), pp. 365–367.

V THE SECOND PHASE
OF THE DEBATE
ON THE PILL

The 1950's saw widespread acceptance of birth regulation as a practical necessity in the lives of most married couples; however, the only method that seemed compatible with Catholic moral principles was the use of rhythm. Quite understandably, then, when the anovulant pill first appeared on the scene the initial discussion of its use centered to a large extent on its relationship to rhythm. Its morality was judged primarily in terms of the help it offered to married couples in making rhythm a safe and manageable method of family planning.

NEW FACTORS

In the 1960's new factors began to enter the picture and widen the areas of discussion. Chief, perhaps, among these factors was the gradual disillusionment of many married couples whose experience brought them to the conclusion that rhythm, even when it proved to be a workable means of family planning, tended seriously to disrupt the interpersonal love relationship of husband and wife. The long periods of abstinence required for its effective use all too often produced frustration, irritability and even estrangement that imperiled the harmony and stability of married life and the family. Many came to feel that the good achieved by rhythm was being purchased at too high a price. In much of the Roman Catholic literature on the subject, rhythm was presented as the "natural" method of birth con-

trol; yet to many couples it seemed anything but "natural." Rosemary
Ruether articulated the feelings of many when she wrote in the December, 1963, issue of *Jubilee:*

The rhythm method is natural only in a restricted sense of the word. . . .
To say that a husband and wife are acting "naturally" when by the most
elaborate tabulations and contrivances, with a bristling arsenal of thermom-
eters and sugar tapes, and resorting to precautions like sleeping in different
beds or in different rooms, they manage to restrict their lovemaking to
times of sterility, but acting "unnaturally" when they prevent the meeting
of egg and sperm by mechanical or medical means, seems a rather one-
sided use of the word "natural."[1]

This growing feeling that rhythm, in perhaps the majority of cases,
was not an adequate solution to the problem of responsible parenthood was accompanied by an effort to probe more deeply into the
meaning of responsible parenthood itself. The term had only recently
become acceptable in Roman Catholic theology. What precisely did
it mean? Certainly it meant at least: (1) the exclusion of any contraceptive mentality which would shun the responsibility of parenthood for purely selfish reasons, and (2) a reasonable and prudent
openness in a marriage to the generation of offspring. But did it also
mean that every act of intercourse must be open to conception?
There were those who concluded that it did not. They believed that a
legitimate distinction could be drawn between the fertility of a marriage and the fertility of a particular instance of sexual union. The
former was an essential element of any responsible approach to
parenthood; the latter was not.

Closely connected with this effort to define more clearly the meaning of responsible parenthood was yet a third factor that helped
broaden the discussion of birth control in the Roman Catholic community. This was the growing conviction that heretofore Roman
Catholic theology on marriage had often tended to overemphasize
biological values at the expense of personal values. This lack of
balance had to be corrected, for intercourse is much more than a

biological function; it is a human act with deep psychological implications for a man and woman. To make biological finality the sole or even the most important criterion of the morality of intercourse seemed, therefore, a distortion of the personalist dimension in married life. A proper appreciation of the personal values in marriage would include recognition of the need, at times, to subordinate the biological finality of intercourse to the human values. If rhythm proved inadequate to serve this need, then other forms of birth regulation that would safeguard the priority of these human values would be permissible.

Two Mentalities

In the light of these new factors, two mentalities emerged to become the focus of much of the current discussion on birth control in the Roman Catholic Church. Adherents of both points of view agreed on the necessity of going beyond rhythm in order to find a satisfactory solution to the problem of family planning.

One group distinguished between permissible methods of contraception and those that were not permitted, maintaining that the malice of contraception consisted not in the positive and deliberate exclusion of procreation, but in the perversion of the marital sex act. Contraceptive methods such as use of the pill would be permitted when there was serious reason for employing them; those contraceptive methods which perverted the natural integrity of the sex act would be forbidden.

Other theologians were not satisfied with this approach. While conceding that it faced more honestly the limitations of rhythm and offered a more realistic understanding of responsible parenthood, they nevertheless felt that it represented a mentality still caught up in the "biologism" that seemed to undervalue the human and personal dimensions of married life. They preferred to view marriage as a totality and to judge the morality of individual acts, not in isolation, but in the context of that totality. They were of the opinion, therefore, that it might be necessary, in the context of the total picture, to exclude the particular value of procreation from certain acts of intercourse. This would be morally permissible if the reason for doing so was sufficiently serious and if the overall plan of marriage included the intention of having children. In such a case, husband and wife would choose the method of birth control which they considered most compatible with considerate behavior and a true expression of their love for one another.

This brief summary suggests the general lines of thought that developed and were much debated during the period between 1963 and the publication five years later of *Humanae Vitae*. The following pages will attempt to detail the gradual evolution of these lines of thought as they developed in the Roman Catholic community.

DR. ROCK'S BOOK

The "new debate" on the birth control issue which began in 1963 was touched off by the publication in April of that year of a book entitled *The Time Has Come*, written by a Catholic who was not a theologian but a layman—Dr. John Rock, professor emeritus at Harvard University, a physician who had played a major role in the development of the anovulant pill.

Two years earlier, in an article written for *Good Housekeeping* magazine,[2] Dr. Rock had expressed the hope that the oral contraceptive pill would prove acceptable to his Church; in the same article, however, he had admitted that the Catholic moralists who had thus far expressed themselves on the pill did not share his views.

Indeed they had not. In 1961 there was no indication that any Catholic moralist would have approved the use of the pill for contraceptive purposes. In fact, Dr. Rock's article met with severe criticism. John J. Lynch described it as a typical example of certain "theologically misleading lucubrations" which attempted to reconcile the doctrinal differences in Catholic and non-Catholic thinking on the matter of contraception. Such attempts were doomed to failure because the use of the pill for directly contraceptive purposes was, in the words of Father Lynch, "theologically a closed issue. . . . If there is one decisive answer which can and must be given relative to the anovulant drugs, it is an unqualified negative to the question as to whether they may licitly be used as a means to prevent conception's resulting from conjugal intercourse."[3]

Seemingly undaunted by the adverse criticism evoked by his article, Dr. Rock reasserted his position at greater length in *The Time Has Come*. The time which Rock felt had come was the time for Catholics and non-Catholics to resolve their differences on the matter of birth control. His hopes in this connection may have been premature, but in 1963 the time had come when his position could at least be given a more sympathetic hearing in the Catholic Church than had been possible in 1961. The reason for this was that by the time his book appeared the first session of the Second Vatican Council had already been held. Pope John XXIII had "opened the windows" and the winds of change had begun to stir within the Church. The time had come when long established positions in doctrinal and moral matters were open to examination, to scrutiny and even, when necessary in the light of the Gospel and the needs of the time, to reevaluation and reformulation.

In his book Dr. Rock covered wide areas of the subject of birth regulation—the population problem, public policy and biological research on birth control, and the emerging theology of responsible parenthood in the Catholic Church. But the main thrust of the work was to show that the half-century of strife over birth control in the United States could be resolved by the Catholic Church's acceptance of the progesterone pill as a morally permissible form of birth regulation.

Dr. Rock was aware, of course, that the Church condemned artificial birth control but he did not believe that the progesterone pill, if properly understood, should fall under that condemnation. The pills, he pointed out, could not be described in any true sense of the term as an artificial means of birth control because they involved neither a mechanical device nor a chemical action alien to the bodily processes. Rather than artificial, they were a physiological means of birth control. They prevented reproduction "by modifying the time sequences in the body's own functions."[4] Physiologically, they simply duplicated what took place in rhythm, since the use of rhythm "depends precisely on the secretion of progesterone from the ovaries." It is progesterone which prevents ovulation and establishes the pre- and postmenstrual safe period that makes the use of rhythm workable. The pill made it possible for man to do by his own reason and in an entirely predictable way what was done naturally, but much less predictably, by the unthinking organs of the body. The pills, therefore, did not represent an artificial intrusion against nature but involved, rather, a cooperation with natural processes.

In the light of this understanding, Dr. Rock asked whether it was semantically correct to stigmatize as temporary sterilization the condition produced by the pill. He preferred to call it "the deferment of the reproductive function" or even the "conservation" of that function, for when the pill is used, "the ova, instead of maturing to a condition where they must die if they are not fertilized, will rest in the ovary to become available when, on omission of medication, nature calls them forth."[5]

The Reaction of American Catholic Moralists

Dr. Rock was obviously enthusiastic about the pill and optimistic about the possibility of its acceptance by the Catholic Church. His optimism was not shared, however, by the American Catholic moralists who responded to his book. Joseph S. Duhamel, writing in *America,* insisted that the same principles which demanded the condemnation of contraception and direct sterilization applied with equal force to the anovulant pill when it was used to suppress ovulation in order to prevent conception. Discounting Rock's basic argument concerning the naturalness of the pill's operation, Father Duhamel said: "It is something of a lyric leap to conclude that, because nature itself inhibits ovulation during pregnancy, therefore it is morally legitimate to inhibit ovulation at other times by deliberately taking oral steroids for that purpose."[6]

Father John J. Lynch wrote in the same vein:

The fact that nature, on the occasion of pregnancy, makes provisions for a concomitant anovulatory period simply does not warrant the conclusion that one is therefore morally entitled to anticipate nature by including that same effect in non-pregnant women by artificial means. Denial of our right to do precisely that is of the very essence of Catholic teaching on direct sterilization. It is quite obvious, for example, that death from natural causes is a very common occurrence. But that biological fact does not justify one's anticipating nature in this respect by deliberately and directly terminating innocent human life, even by means which might duplicate nature's own lethal processes. In the disposal of our lives or of our bodies and their functions, we are not always morally free to imitate nature.[7]

Fathers John C. Ford of the Catholic University of America and Gerald Kelly were also unmoved by Dr. Rock's defense of contraception through the use of the pill. They said: "We can state that Dr. Rock's opinions in this matter have no standing whatever with Catholic theologians and directly contravene the authoritative teaching of the Catholic Church which is binding on all Catholics."[8]

European Reactions

While certain American theologians were confidently asserting the unanimity of theological opposition to Dr. Rock's position, there were indications that in Europe Dr. Rock's approach was receiving serious and sympathetic consideration.

Bishop William Bekkers

On March 21, 1963—just one month prior to the publication of *The Time Has Come*—William Bekkers, Bishop of the diocese of Don

Bosch in Holland, gave a talk on television in which he spoke of marriage in terms strongly personalist and existential. He pointed out that modern science, by making it possible for man to regulate reproduction, had brought family planning within the scope of human responsibility. Man therefore had to accept the responsibility of birth regulation as a normal part of the overall plan of married life, and it had to be a truly personal responsibility assumed by a married couple.

From within their human experience of marriage, that is, out of their love and responsibility for each other, for their procreative powers, and for the family that already exists, the married couple—and they alone—can answer the question of what God requires of them concretely in their vocation. They must decide how large their family should be, and how their children should be spaced. . . . This is a matter for their own consciences with which nobody should interfere.[9]

It was only in this context of the total responsibility of married life, the Bishop said, that methods of birth regulation could be rightly discussed. The rhythm method seemed to afford the best answer to the problem of birth regulation according to the Catholic point of view, yet even this method was not above criticism. While it might have been a solution for many people, it created insurmountable obstacles for many others. These serious difficulties in the practical order could not be ignored when a judgment was being made on methods of birth regulation.

We can understand that there are situations in which people find themselves unable to fulfill all their Christian ideals and human values at the same time. The Church does not judge situations from a prejudiced, aloof point of view . . . it knows that what may be attainable for one individual is not necessarily so for another.[10]

Bishop Bekkers invited the priests and people of his diocese to offer comments on his talk. Some of those commenting suggested that his statement had been too vague, that it had stressed personal responsibility but had offered no practical solutions. In a subsequent statement the Bishop admitted the validity of the criticism, but suggested that the "vagueness" of his statement was due, not to unwillingness to speak concretely, but to the ambiguity of the topic with which he dealt. The Church was in a state of "knowing, yet not knowing" regarding a number of issues, and one of these, he felt, was the progesterone pill. The traditional arguments against contraception were well-known, but uncertainty still existed as to whether they applied to the pill. In the Bishop's opinion, certain theologians had been too hasty in making sweeping statements about the morality of the pill which ignored the fact that it operated in a way different from other well-known contraceptives. The question required more study. Bishop Bekkers suggested, "At least some limitations of phrasing are necessary, such as 'as far as we can judge now. . . . Another idea may not be impossible in the near future.' "[11]

Oversimplified explanations, expressed in abstract categorical statements, could sometimes be dangerously out of touch with concrete reality.

The Dutch Hierarchy

On August 10, 1963, six months after the publication of Dr. Rock's book, the Dutch bishops issued the first official statement by a national hierarchy on the question of the pill. Their statement was in substantial agreement with Bishop Bekker's position. Expressing their own deep concern for the problems that beset the faithful, they pointed out that in the last resort personal conscience, listening to the divine law and taking notice of the Church's interpretation of that law, must give the decisive verdict.[12] At the same time, they admitted a certain ambiguity in the understanding of divine law. New views of men and human sexuality, they said, together with newly developed scientific means of birth regulation, had presented the Church with questions for which "she has no immediately appropriate answer ready that meets all situations."[13] The bishops, therefore, expressed the hope that these questions would be discussed in a broader context at the second session of the Council. Meanwhile, they said that while it was clear that oral contraceptives could no more be accepted as a general solution to the problem of birth regulation than the contraceptive devices already known, "Catholic moral theologians are discussing the question of whether these means could be accepted in certain circumstances."[14]

Canon Louis Janssens

Canon Louis Janssens of Louvain was one of the moral theologians exploring this precise question. He expressed his substantial support of Dr. Rock's position in a lengthy article in the October-December 1963 issue of *Ephemerides Theologicae Lovanienses.* He questioned the generally accepted position that the progesterone pill could be used only for therapeutic purposes, and attempted to demonstrate that, morally speaking, there was no essential difference between the use of the pill and the practice of rhythm.

In the practice of rhythm, he wrote, two elements were involved that had to be considered in determining its morality. First, there was the deliberate suppression of the generative function accomplished by a careful calculation of *time:* the time of the release of the ovum, the time the spermatozoa retain their fertilizing power, the time required for the ovum to disintegrate.

All these calculations show quite well that a *temporal* obstacle is intentionally being placed in the way of the ovum's performing its reproductive function (just as the use of mechanical methods or of *coitus interruptus* places a *spatial* obstacle for the same purpose.[15]

Rhythm, in other words, did not simply involve the non-use of the generative faculties during the time of fertility; it also involved the use of a particular act of intercourse at a definite time, i.e., at a time known to be infertile. There was therefore in the use of rhythm, not only the intention of excluding procreation but also the choice of a particular act as a means of accomplishing this intention. Accordingly, the conclusion could be drawn that the decisive reason for condemning the use of contraceptive devices could not lie in the positive and deliberate use of some means of excluding procreation from the marital act because this was precisely what happened in the use of rhythm.

In addition to this filtering out of the procreative aspect of intercourse, there was another element in rhythm which was crucial in determining its morality, namely, the intrinsic structure of the act of intercourse was preserved intact. This, in the final analysis, was the reason why the use of rhythm could be justified, whereas the use of contraceptive devices could not. The latter destroyed the natural structure of the marital act and were therefore morally objectionable.[16]

The pill, Janssens maintained, belonged in the same moral category as rhythm. While its use involved a positive and deliberate exclusion of procreation (as did rhythm), at the same time it preserved intact the intrinsic structure of the act of intercourse (again, as did rhythm). Janssens concluded, therefore, that the use of the pill was as morally unobjectionable as the practice of rhythm.

Janssens foresaw that some, taking their lead from the words of Pius XII in 1958, might argue that the use of the pill amounted to direct temporary sterilization and for that reason was morally wrong. He discounted this objection by suggesting that the essence of sterilization is the destruction of the reproductive faculty, even though it is in good health, in order to make procreation impossible. The pill did not destroy the reproductive faculty or eliminate the possibility of future procreation. It simply deferred or delayed the carrying out of that function.

Canon Janssens concluded his article on a practical, pastoral note:

One must not have recourse to the use of progestogene when periodic continence is possible and sufficiently efficient to assure voluntary and generous procreation. . . . (But) when periodic continence is not practicable or is insufficiently efficient . . . it seems to us that it could be replaced by recourse to progestogenes, as long as they are used in the service of a justified birth regulation.[17]

Reactions to Janssens' Article

Janssens' departure from the widely accepted view that the pill could be used only for therapeutic reasons received support in the writings of several European theologians. William H. van der Marck, professor at the Catholic University of Nijmigen, and the Most Reverend J. M. Reuss, auxiliary bishop of Mainz in Germany, though arguing from a different point of view, arrived at the same conclusion as Canon Janssens: the pill could be used as a legitimate means of family limitation.[18]

In America, however, the reaction to Janssens' article was quite different. Father Edward Duff reported in the *Religious News Service:* "Father Janssens' professional peers in the United States promptly rejected his arguments as specious and as adding nothing to the rejected claims of Dr. Rock."[19] The promptness and vigor of the reaction in America moved *Time* magazine to comment: "Catholic moralists in the United States reacted to the article as if Canon Janssens had nailed a 96th thesis to the door of Wittenberg Castle."[20] Msgr. Salvatore J. Adamo, editor of the *Camden Star Herald,* the first newspaper in the United States to publish Janssens' article, declared that the article provoked near hysteria in some Catholic newspapers and magazines, "as though a theologian had suddenly come out in favor of sin."[21]

The strongest opposition came from those Catholic moralists who for more than a decade had exercised the unofficial roles of Catholic spokesmen on the American moral scene: Fathers John J. Lynch, John C. Ford, Gerald Kelly, and Francis J. Connell of the Catholic University of America, Washington, D.C.

Father Connell stated: "Any method used to frustrate the generative power of the conjugal act is absolutely wrong and a violation of the principles involved in the Church's teaching on marriage."[22] In the opinion of Father Lynch, Janssens' stand was "totally invalid

and impossible to reconcile with present theological principles."[23]
Father Ford, appealing to the papal statement of 1958, declared:

Unless and until the Holy See gives its approval to some other teaching (a
highly unlikely eventuality), no lesser authority in the Church, and least
of all a private theologian, is at liberty to teach a different doctrine or to
free Catholics from their obligation to accept a papal teaching.[24]

In a similar statement, Father Kelly said:

Sound pastoral policy requires us to abide by the clear teaching of Pius XI
and Pius XII. According to this teaching, the use of contraceptive tech-
niques and the suppression of normal generative function as means of
rendering the conjugal act infertile are intrinsically immoral. The contraceptive use of the pill is explicitly included in this teaching; such use of
the pill is also intrinsically immoral.[25]

An editorial in *America* summarized the attitude of many American
Catholic moralists. Declaring that Janssens' argument was not likely
to convince anyone who was not already eager to be convinced, the
editorial continued:

Periodic continence, as its name proclaims, "prevents" conception by abstinence, that is, by the *non*-performance of the conjugal act during the fertile
period. The pill prevents conception by suppressing ovulation and by thus
abolishing the fertile period. No amount of word juggling can make abstinence from sexual relations and the suppression of ovulation one and the
same thing. If Canon Janssens wants to enlighten Catholic thinking on the
pill, he will have to come up with a better argument.[26]

Yet already in 1964 there were signs of a break in the apparent
unanimity among American Catholic theologians on the birth control
issue. Younger moral theologians, just beginning to break into print,
showed themselves more open to new insights and new approaches,
and more willing to face the possibility of a reevaluation of traditional
principles. Father Charles E. Curran, later to become professor of
moral theology at the Catholic University of America, in a carefully
written article in *Jubilee* attempted to set the birth control controversy

in the wider context of an integral view of marriage, its values, and its concrete problems.[27] While his article stopped short of full endorsement of the positions taken by Janssens, van der Marck, and Reuss, his obvious sympathy with their approach seemed to suggest Father Curran's substantial agreement with them. Another American moralist, Father Felix F. Cardegna, professor at Woodstock College, Woodstock, Maryland, in a lengthy summary of the debate on the pill, concluded with the hope that "the use of the pill as proposed by Janssens will be allowed by the Church, at least as a probable view among theologians and permissible in practice."[28]

NOTES

1. Rosemary Ruether, "Marriage, Love, Children," *Jubilee* 11 (December, 1963), p. 19.

2. John Rock, "We Can End the Battle over Birth Control" *Good Housekeeping* (July, 1961), pp. 44–45; 107–109.

3. John J. Lynch, "Notes on Moral Theology," *Theological Studies* 23 (June, 1962), p. 242.

4. John Rock, *The Time Has Come* (Avon Books. New York: Alfred A. Knopf, Inc., 1963), p. 149.

5. Rock, *The Time Has Come,* p. 152.

6. Joseph S. Duhamel, "The Time Has Come" (a review), *America* 108 (April, 27, 1963), p. 610.

7. John J. Lynch, "The Time Has Come" (a review), *Marriage* 45 (June, 1963), pp. 16–17.

8. John C. Ford and Gerald Kelly, *Contemporary Moral Theology,* Vol. 2. See footnote, pp. 376–377.

9. W. M. Bekkers, *God's People on the March* (New York: Holt, Rinehart & Winston, Inc., 1966), pp. 114–115.

10. *Op. cit.,* p. 116.

11. *Op. cit.,* p. 119.

12. "Statement of the Dutch Bishops," quoted in Leo Pyle, ed., *The Pill and Birth Regulation* (Baltimore, Md., Helicon Press, Inc., 1964), p. 33.

13. *Op. cit.,* p. 34.

14. *Ibid.*

15. Louis Janssens, "Morale conjugale et progestogenes," *Ephemerides Theologicae Lovanienses* 39 (October-December, 1963), p. 822, quoted in Felix F.

Cardegna, "Contraception, the Pill and Responsible Parenthood," *Theological Studies* 25 (December, 1964), pp. 618–619.

16. *Op. cit.,* quoted in Pyle, *op. cit.,* p. 17.

17. *Op. cit.,* quoted in Pyle, *op. cit.,* pp. 18–19.

18. William H. van der Marck, *Love and Fertility* (London: Sheed and Ward Ltd., 1965), pp. 1–105; J. M. Reuss, "Mutual Love and Procreation," *Tubinger Theologischen Quartalschrift* 143 (1963), pp. 454–476.

19. Edward Duff, "Moral Experts Divide on the Pill," *Rochester Courier Journal,* March 6, 1964.

20. "A New View on Birth Control," *Time* (April 10, 1964), p. 59.

21. Salvatore J. Adamo, "The Pill and the Press," *Camden Star Herald,* April 3, 1964.

22. "U.S. Theologians Hit Endorsement of the Pill," *The* (St. Paul) *Catholic Bulletin,* March 6, 1964, quoted in Francis Swift, "An Analysis of the American Theological Reaction to Janssens' Stand on the Pill," *Louvain Studies* 1 (Fall, 1966), p. 22.

23. *Ibid.*

24. John C. Ford, quoted in Pyle, *op. cit.,* p. 22.

25. Gerald Kelly, "Confusion: Contraception and the Pill," *Theology Digest* 12 (Summer, 1964), p. 124.

26. "Time's Bomb," *America* (April 25, 1964), p. 563.

27. Charles E. Curran, "Christian Marriage and Family Planning," *Jubilee* 12 (August, 1964), pp. 8–13.

28. Felix F. Cardegna, "Contraception, the Pill, and Responsible Parenthood," *Theological Studies* 25 (December, 1964), p. 636.

VI THE WIDENING OF THE BIRTH CONTROL DEBATE

By 1964 it was evident that there had been a rift in the unanimity of teaching regarding the progesterone pill; equally evident was the fact that the debate on birth control could no longer be limited to discussions of rhythm or even the pill. The point had been passed when it was enough to say that rhythm was morally permissible because it was not contraception, or that the pill could be justified when its use was not contraceptive.

The issue that had been waiting in the wings for so long a time was finally forced onto center stage: the issue of contraception itself. Suddenly many Catholics—laity, clergy, and bishops—were asking the question that was at the heart of the matter: why was contraception wrong? The question, of course, had been asked in 1930, and the answer given at the time had presumably settled the matter once and for all. But now, thirty-four years later, it seemed almost a new question. It had acquired a new context because large segments of the Catholic community entertained serious intellectual doubts about the validity of the 1930 answer; they were no longer disposed to accept it as definitive and irrevocable. John J. Lynch, writing in *Theological Studies* in June, 1965, reviewed recent literature in the field of moral theology and admitted:

It is now common knowledge for the world at large that Catholic doctrine with regard to contraception in general, and more particularly with respect to the oral contraceptives, is being questioned at almost every level within the Church. Cardinals, bishops, ordained theologians and other priests, trained philosophers and theologians among our articulate laymen, harried husbands and wives—virtually every echelon within the Church is represented in an interrogative chorus whose voices range from the stridently emotional to the rationally insistent. It would be irrelevant, even if it were not impossible, to determine exactly what percentage of theologians throughout the world entertain sincere intellectual doubts with regard to our traditional theology of contraception. The practical fact of the matter is that any literate Catholic at the present time can recite a litany of authorities, whether real or alleged, who have publicly expressed such doubts.[1]

It was an article published in April, 1964, in *Search,* the liberal British Catholic newsletter, that exploded the contraceptive issue in many directions. What attracted special attention to the article was the fact that it was written by a Roman Catholic archbishop, Thomas D. Roberts, S.J., the former Archbishop of Bombay who had resigned his See in favor of a native Indian bishop and who had already earned a reputation for espousing unpopular causes.

In his *Search* article, the Archbishop questioned the rational basis of the entire Catholic position on contraception. He articulated a growing sentiment among many Catholics when he stated, with characteristic bluntness, that he personally could not follow "what is called the ethical argument. It does not seem to me to be conclusive." He continued:

If I were not a Catholic, I would accept the position taken by the Lambeth Conference, namely, that there are cases when conscientious thought by the parties concerned would entitle people to practice contraception. How you can destroy the position by reason alone is not clear to me.[2]

But Archbishop Roberts *was* a Catholic and the Catholic Church has always taught that contraception is morally wrong. The Archbishop declared, therefore, that he accepted the Church's present teaching only because of her authority. Yet, he pointed out, the argument from authority presented its own difficulty, since the Church did not simply say that contraception was wrong; she said that it was wrong precisely because it was against the natural law. In other words, the Church based her position not on an argument from revelation, but on the ethical argument. Archbishop Roberts, and with him an increasing number of Catholics, thus found himself in the exceedingly uncomfortable situation of being asked, not simply to accept the condemnation of contraception on the authority of the Church, but on the basis of that authority to accept as well the very argument which he had already rejected on the basis of reason. In view of this dilemma, Archbishop Roberts urged that the Council take up the entire question of the relation of natural law to contraception.

> Those of us [he wrote] who cannot see why or how to convict of crime the millions who see contraception as a right or duty in marriage . . . certainly may and must press for the acceptance by the General Council of the "challenge" to justify by reason our own challenge to the world made in the name of reason.[3]

The article shook the Catholic world. Widely reported and discussed, it was the kind of statement that many had hoped—and some had feared—would come.

There was an almost immediate official reaction within the Catholic Church in England. Father Maurice O'Leary, chairman of the Catholic Marriage Advisory Council, issued a statement on April 24, 1964. Noting the growing concern among priests and people about rumors of possible changes in the Church's teaching on contraception, he said: "There is no uncertainty about the Church's teaching on contraception. From earliest times until today it has been condemned. . . . We have this certainty from the teaching of the Church that contraception is intrinsically immoral and no opinion to the contrary may be followed."[4]

He admitted, however, that it was not to be inferred from the Church's teaching on contraception that "the arguments in favor of it from reason alone are clear and immediately conclusive."[5] In fact, he stated, the reason why God had given us the Church as a teacher in faith and morals was "precisely to provide the certainty and security that one would not have if left to unaided reason."[6]

Auberon Waugh, a regular columnist of the *Catholic Herald,* offered the comment that Maurice O'Leary might have been right in saying that there was no uncertainty in the past over the Church's attitude toward contraception but "if the Church includes its present members on earth there is plainly quite a bit of uncertainty."[7]

Father O'Leary's statement was the prelude to an official statement issued by the then Archbishop John Heenan in the name of the bishops of England and Wales. The statement spoke of the bishops' duty to proclaim the unchanging nature of God's law—a duty made all the more pressing because imprudent statements had been made questioning the Church's competence and sowing doubts in the minds of the faithful. While admitting that the Council might be called upon to make a pronouncement on the anovulant pill, the bishops insisted in unambiguous terms that contraception itself "is not an open question, for it is against the law of God."[8]

For several weeks the British papers were flooded with letters to the editor commenting on Archbishop Robert's article, Maurice O'Leary's statement and the statement of the hierarchy. Some of the writers expressed puzzlement at the contrast between the clarity of the Church's stand on contraception (as set forth by O'Leary's statement and that of the hierarchy) and the ambiguity of the reasons from natural law used to substantiate that stand. One of the letters said that Archbishop Roberts had given a glimmer of hope to Catholic laymen who find themselves "constantly disillusioned by their own and the Church's inability to defend rationally her attitude on this vital question."[9] A Mr. P. Glazebrook expressed agreement with Archbishop Roberts that Catholic teaching on contraception was "unreasonable." Catholic parents, he suggested, who have to put this teaching into practice, "are entitled to better and more logical reasons than those recently given in the Catholic press."[10]

Other letters pleaded the need for a major development of the Church's teaching, not simply on contraception but on the whole doctrine of marriage. Norman St. John-Stevas, a Catholic lawyer and Member of Parliament, wrote:

Theological and social pressures are jointly responsible for the present ferment. Many Catholic theologians are unhappy about the stark Augustinian teaching on marriage which has for so long dominated the textbooks on moral theology in use in Catholic seminaries. . . . They want to get away from the biological approach to marriage, with its emphasis on its social and procreative purposes, and reemphasize the vital importance of the personal factors of love, friendship, and union between the spouses.[11]

A letter to the *London Tablet* on May 9, 1964, pointed out what was to become a new dimension of the birth control debate that theologians could not afford to ignore, namely, the growing discontent of young people within the Church. The rising generation, he said, simply would not accept the Church's teaching in this matter "if it remains unmodified in the light of recent discoveries."[12]

Symptomatic of this discontent of the young with the theological debate on birth control was the letter of a Catholic girl who was shortly to be married. With the characteristic impatience of youth, she brushed aside theological differences in favor of a personalist understanding of the relationship of husband and wife. Writing of her fiancé and herself, she said:

We both believe that the expression of our love should be natural and spontaneous, not for our own sexual satisfaction, but to provide a harmonious and happy background for the family we shall have. We feel self-control should be used with mutual respect and consideration. If this cannot be done without the use of contraceptives, then contraceptives should be used.[13]

By this time Rome had already stepped into the birth control controversy—first, in the person of Cardinal Alfredo Ottaviani, Prefect of the Holy Office, and then by the Pope himself. What Rome said seemed restrained and undefinitive. Cardinal Ottaviani, in an interview which first appeared in the Italian journal *Vita*, expressed his conviction that the Supreme Magisterium must speak "in grave and debatable questions."[14] Such questions should not be left to the opinion of individuals, he said, even though those individuals were bishops or cardinals. He recommended that those who had something to say on the matter of birth control should refer their ideas to the Pope so that he might have before him all the relevant considerations.

Pope Paul's entry into the controversy came, as we have seen in Chapter II, on June 23, 1964, when he announced to a gathering of cardinals that the Pontifical Study Commission on Family, Population, and Birth Problems was engaged in a thorough and broadly based study of the entire question of birth control. He hoped, he said, to be able soon to announce the conclusions of that study. To-date, however, there was insufficient reason for considering as outdated or not binding the norms given by Pius XII, and therefore these norms must be regarded as valid, "at least until we feel obliged in conscience to change them."[15]

Again as we have seen previously, those who had hoped for a change in the Church's teaching on contraception found grounds for that hope in the papal statement, maintaining that it conceded the mutability of the Church's position. Others did not see that the Church's position was in any way weakened by the Pope's words. They claimed that the Pope had neither affirmed nor denied the *de facto* mutability of the teaching of Pius XII; he had simply expressed, without implying any doubt on his part, his willingness to let experts in various fields put that teaching to the test.

AFTER THE PAPAL STATEMENT

On one point, at least, those who opposed change seemed to be in agreement with those who favored it: the natural law arguments against contraception were inconclusive. According to John J. Lynch, it was quite unlikely that a formulation of these arguments would ever achieve "that degree of clarity required to convince all of its cogency."[16] He felt that those who were convinced of the evil of contraception had to rely almost exclusively on the "theological approach, which appeals to an uninterrupted tradition of ecclesiastical doctrine culminating in the solemn declaration voiced by Pius XI in *Casti Connubii*."[17]

Gerald Kelly pointed out what he considered the limitations of any discussion of the natural law arguments against contraception. "We, as Catholic theologians, are not studying this matter in order to find the truth. We already have it. We know from the teaching of the Church that contraception is intrinsically immoral."[18]

Nonetheless, he agreed that the Catholic theologian should study the relationship of contraception to the natural law—first, in order to gain a more profound insight into Catholic teaching and, secondly, in order to show fellow-Catholics and others the reasonableness of the Church's condemnation of contraception.

In another article, Father Kelly admitted that the rational arguments against contraception were not always easy to follow; nevertheless, he was confident that "we already have strong arguments on rational grounds for the Catholic position."[19] The principal argument, he said, was that outlined by the popes—that contraception infringed on the inviolable divine plan for the beginning of human life, and the natural structure of intercourse is a part of that plan which man is not free to change. He also pointed out that some theologians had recently emphasized that contraception violated not only the primary purpose of marriage, i.e., its orientation to new life, but also its secondary purposes, for it placed an obstacle in the way which impeded the total and unreserved self-giving and the complete mutual acceptance on the part of husband and wife that intercourse implies. Father Kelly concluded with some optimism that "the rational case against contraception is much stronger than the arguments adduced for it."[20]

Not all moralists who supported the Church's ban on contraception shared Father Kelly's optimistic evaluation of the strength of the arguments used to defend the Church's position; nor were they content to rely as heavily as Lynch and Kelly on the argument from authority. They felt that the natural law arguments were inconclusive, not because reason could not prove that contraception was wrong, but because the reasons used in the past were inadequate. They believed that philosophical reasoning was capable of producing convincing proof that contraception was immoral.

Germain G. Grisez, associate professor of philosophy at Georgetown University in Washington, D.C., presented such a philosophical approach in *Contraception and the Natural Law*. Dr. Grisez set his discussion of the contraceptive issue within the broader perspective of a general theory of ethics. The conclusions he drew were traditional; his reasons for arriving at these conclusions were not.

╱ He began with an evaluation and rejection of the traditional argument against contraception: that it is intrinsically evil because it prevents the act of intercourse from attaining its natural end. His main objection was that the word "natural" was used in an ambiguous and equivocal sense.[21] The argument thus moved, unjustifiably, from the observable level of physiological finality to the level of moral obligation, inferring what *ought to be* from what *is*. In short, the defect in the argument was that it failed to prove that the natural end of the act implied a moral obligation.

Grisez followed his rejection of the traditional argumentation with a presentation of his own ethical theory. He began with the notion of practical reason as the source of moral obligation, saying: "The first prescription of practical reason is that good should be pursued and that actions appropriate in that pursuit should be done, and also that actions which are not helpful in the pursuit of the good or which interfere with it should be avoided."[22]

He then asked the question: What are the goods, worthy of man's pursuit, to which practical reason can direct human actions? Instead of attempting to give an exhaustive list of these basic human goods, he indicated those of life, truth, freedom, and procreation. At first principles, they cannot be demonstrated; yet since men, in fact, do pursue them, they can legitimately be postulated. They are part of the radical, rational constitution of man.

These basic goods, Grisez continued, make several demands on man. He must always take them into account by respecting them and being sensitive to the human possibilities which they establish. This does not mean that man must always be acting toward them; what it does mean is that he can never, with direct intent, act against their realization, for to do so would be intrinsically evil.

Grisez applied this general theory of ethics to the problem of contraception: procreation was a basic human good which man need not always seek but which he must never deliberately prevent. Therefore, the malice of contraception does not lie in the violation of any general rule to cause conception but rather in placing one's self "directly against the essential good of procreation," and "in an absurd conflict between an unavoidable volition of that good and a free volition against it."[23] To act against procreation, therefore, is to act against man's rational nature, for it involves "the direct violation of the procreative good as a value in itself, as an ideal which never may be submerged. He who practices contraception acts directly against one of the principles which makes human action meaningful."[24]

The existence of diverse opinions in the philosophy department at Georgetown was amply evidenced by the sharp critique of Grisez' position written by Dr. Louis Dupré, also an associate professor of philosophy there. Dr. Dupré suggested that his colleague's keen awareness of the defects of the traditional theories of natural law was, unfortunately, not matched by a similar incisiveness in presenting his own theory. Grisez had proved that a basic principle of the moral law does have the procreative good as its object; what he had not proved was that it is necessarily a good in all cases. He assumed that "to have intercourse is to place oneself in the situation of procreation and that the obligation to promote the procreative good follows directly from this procreative situation."[25] But, Dupré objected, procreation in certain cases is not a good; hence there is no obligation to promote it. Moreover, Grisez' position was based on the supposition that "the sexual act has no other essential meaning than to promote procreation."[26] This, Dupré maintained, was obviously false, "since the fulfillment of love is equally essential to the marital act."[27]

THE REVISIONISTS

Prior to his critique of Grisez' book, Dr. Dupré had already expressed his views on the contraceptive issue. Indeed, he had been largely responsible for initiating open discussion of the subject among American Catholics. His articles in *Commonweal*[28] and *Cross Currents*[29] helped to achieve on the American scene what Archbishop Roberts' *Search* article had done in England: they shifted the birth control debate from the issue of the pill to the broader problem of contraception itself. The views set forth in those two articles were restated in fuller form in his book *Contraception and Catholics*.

Dupré was one of those who believed that Catholic teaching on marriage had to be rescued from the biologism that had characterized it since Augustine's time and placed in a total human context. Like Grisez, he took issue with the common argument based on natural law but his approach and his conclusion were quite different from those of Grisez.

As generally stated, the argument against contraception is based on the inviolability of the marital act and starts with the major premise that it is evil to separate an act from its natural end; hence the use of contraceptives is always evil. The difficulty that Dupré found with this kind of reasoning was its failure to distinguish between the intrinsic finality of nature as a whole and the individual act of intercourse. As he put it: "The intrinsic finality of nature must be actualized if nature is to continue its existence, but this actualization is not bound to any individual act."[30]

Nature itself, he added, has made ample provision for exceptions in regard to intercourse, since the act does not always, or even generally, attain the end of procreation.

Dupré's strongest objection was to the tendency of the anticontraceptionists to identify man's biological structure with his human nature; once this identification had been made, they then asserted the sacred, inviolable character of human nature. Thus an act against biological finality became an act against nature. Dupré maintained it was wrong to equate man's biological structure with his total human nature, since to do so was to ignore other human values, and to make one value so absolute that it threatened all others.

A married couple, who for good physiological, economic or psychological reasons should have no more children, may find that for them rhythm is ineffective; if we force them to choose either abstinence from intercourse or the near certainty of more children, we impose on them an alternative in which values as essential as love and the well-being of their children are sacrificed. Such a decision would seem to require a more solid justification than reference to the intrinsic finality of man's biological nature.[31]

Dupré also rejected the psychological argument against contraception, which was based not on the natural structure of intercourse but on its fundamental meaning. The act of intercourse, the argument ran, is a symbol of the total self-surrender of husband and wife to one another. Contraception, because it involves calculation and reserve, contradicts that symbolism and therefore destroys the fundamental meaning of the marital act; for this reason, it is intrinsically evil. Against this mentality, Dupré argued that the total gift of self in marriage is not and cannot be made in a single act; it can only be made gradually over a period of time through a series of acts. In other words, man, a being who lives his existence in time, is unable to express himself once and forever in a single act. Dupré concedes that to deprive the marital act permanently and constantly of its tendency toward procreation would imply a basic reservation in self-surrender that would contradict the objective meaning of that act. But, he added:

. . . for two marriage partners who have repeatedly proven their intention of complete surrender in creative acts of love, to exclude occasionally the fertility of their love when circumstances prevent them from taking proper care of new offspring does not necessarily contradict the objective meaning of the marital act. . . . The full meaning of these occasional acts can be grasped only by connecting them with the totality of all others.[32]

The year 1964 saw the publication of several other books which also questioned the absolute prohibition of contraception. *Contraception and Holiness* was a collection of essays written by specialists of various disciplines: philosophy, theology, biology, sociology. Archbishop Roberts' introduction, an expanded version of his earlier article in *Search,* set the book's tone by calling for a reexamination of the Church's position on contraception. The other contributors, each approaching the issue in terms of his own competency, were united in the conviction that the Church's stand on contraception must be modified, and her teaching on marriage reexamined and more adequately expressed. Of particular significance were the essays of two professors of St. Michael's College of the University of Toronto: "Casti Connubii and the Development of Doctrine" by Leslie Dewart and "Can the Church Change Her Position on Birth Control?" by Gregory Baum. Both essays attempted to show that a modification in the Church's attitude toward contraception would represent a genuine doctrinal development of the Church's teaching. Such a development would be faithful to the basic values emphasized in the Church's tradition and enunciated by Pius XI; at the same time it would reveal an openness to newer insights, only recently available, into the place of sexuality in marriage. According to Father Baum:

If the magisterium were to change its position and teach that contraception, while dangerous and not generally commendable, is not *intrinsically* evil and hence permissible on certain occasions, this would be in harmony with a general development of doctrine that has *already* taken place in the Church. The Catholic Church would then continue to proclaim the unchanging value of fruitfulness and selfless love in marriage, but favor an application of this value in a way which leaves more room for human planning. Changing her position on birth control, the Catholic Church would not be unfaithful to her own self-understanding.[33]

One of the ways in which the Church grows in her understanding of the Gospel, Baum contended, is by consulting people who have attempted to live the Gospel. Consequently, the theologian working out a theology of marriage must listen to the Christian witness of married people. Michael Novak offered the theologian just such an opportunity in an unusual book, *The Experience of Marriage*,[34] which grew out of an invitation extended by Mr. Novak to a number of American Catholic married couples. He asked these husbands and wives to articulate this Christian witness in terms of their own experience of married life. Thirteen couples—from a variety of backgrounds, professions and years of married life—responded. The result was a remarkable series of personal stories, some telling of married love reaching the heights of heroism and growing in the process; others of married love stretched thin by strain, frustration, and a gnawing sense of futility. The book left the reader with three overall impressions: (1) that a solution of the birth control problem seemed to be the key to any satisfactory synthesis of the various elements involved in married life, (2) that for the majority of married people rhythm offered anything but a satisfactory solution to the problem, and (3) that many married couples were exasperated and embittered by the apparent unwillingness or inability of so many celibate theologians to view marital sexuality in any terms other than the alternatives of self-indulgence or self-control. The book drew no conclusion, but it forced an issue to the forefront of the reader's mind: The absolute prohibition of contraception, with which Catholic couples are obliged to live, seems to be a principle that in so many cases is destructive of married love and married life. Can it really be a Christian principle?

What Modern Catholics Think about Birth Control,[35] edited by William Birmingham, was published in November, 1964; like *The Experience of Marriage,* it was also written entirely by lay Catholics. Described as a new symposium, the book ranged over a variety of topics related to birth control. The initial essay, by Vernon J. Bourke, was a defense of the traditional Catholic position. In addition to essays on psychiatry and family limitation (Philip R. Sullivan), public policy and birth control (John Leo), sociology and birth control (John J. Kane), natural law and overpopulation (Frederick E.

Flynn), there were discussions of authority, conscience, and freedom (William Birmingham, Rosemary Ruether). There were personal reflections by five married women on such topics as the role of women, the feminine mystique, and family planning.

Michael Novak, in a perceptive essay, "Toward a Positive Sexual Morality," suggested that marital sexuality is on the threshold of a doctrinal development which will not contradict the values embodied in past tradition, but which will take into account much more than that tradition. This development will mean a deeper understanding of intercourse as not simply a discrete, physical act, but as something that has a powerful influence on the quality of the lives of husband and wife. This will require a redefinition of intercourse which will go beyond mere biological or juridical terms; due emphasis will have to be given to the psychological and interpersonal dimensions. It will be necessary to give proper importance to psychological criteria in judging the morality of intercourse. "Chief among these criteria would be the victory of mutual consideration over lust, of friendship over concupiscence, of mutual concern over individual passion, hedonism, or egotism."[36]

Daniel Sullivan's contribution, "A History of Catholic Thinking on Contraception,"[37] was the book's lengthiest essay. The author questioned whether there existed prior to the last three decades an *articulated* tradition condemning contraception. He admitted, however, that the presuppositions of that tradition (an antifeminist mentality and an impersonal nonrelational understanding of sexuality and marriage) found abundant, though not universal, expression in the writings of the Fathers and Doctors of the Church. Sullivan's essay, indeed the main thrust of the entire book, was a plea for a reexamination of these presuppositions.[38]

FOUR COUNCIL SPEECHES

In his introduction to *What Modern Catholics Believe about Birth Control,* William Birmingham lamented the lack of communication

between those who live married life and those who generally teach
and write about the theology of marriage. Married Catholic lay
people, he said, "have made little effort to tell one another—and their
priests—what marriage is about."[39] Two historic days at Vatican
Council II, October 29 and 30, 1964, revealed that at least some married Catholic lay people had communicated with their priests—and
with their bishops; moreover, their words had been taken seriously.

On October 29, the fathers of Vatican II began the long-awaited
discussion of that section of Schema 13, *The Church in the Modern
World,* that dealt with marriage and the family. Four of the Council
fathers spoke on the schema in interventions that displayed a remarkable sensitivity to the hardships that Catholic teaching on birth
control seemed to impose on so many Catholic couples and a deep
concern that the Church reexamine that teaching in the light of new
knowledge and with all the resources available to her.

The first of these speakers was Cardinal Paul-Emile Leger, Archbishop of Montreal. He declared that the holiness of marriage must
be one of the primary preoccupations of the Church because of the
doubts and anxieties about marriage that beset so many people from
different countries and different social conditions. "Many of the faithful," he said, "often among them some of the best, encounter daily
difficulties, search for solutions in accord with their faith, but do not
find comfort in the answers given them."[40]

Much of the difficulty, he said, stemmed from a pessimistic and
negative attitude toward human love, attributable neither to Scripture
nor tradition, but to philosophies of past centuries that have veiled
the importance and legitimacy of conjugal love in marriage. This
attitude must be corrected through a more adequate understanding of
the ends of marriage. Procreation and conjugal love should be presented not as the primary and secondary ends of marriage but as two
ends equally good and holy. Moreover, procreation, governed by
prudence and generosity, should be linked not so much with each
act of intercourse as with the whole state of marriage. In such a context it would be clearly seen that "the intimate union of the spouses

also finds a purpose in love. And this end is truly 'the end of the act itself' (*finis operis*), lawful in itself, even when it is not ordained to procreation."[41]

Such a presentation of marriage and its ends would genuinely reflect the actual experience and understanding of married people, for in marriage "the spouses consider each other not as mere procreators, but as persons loved for their own sakes."[42]

This remarkable speech, drawing so obviously on contemporary theological thought, was followed by an equally moving appeal from Cardinal Leo Suenens, Archbishop of Malines-Brussels, Belgium. Stressing the need for complete openness to the Holy Spirit in order to gain a proper understanding of the Gospel, he asked whether the Church had always maintained in perfect balance all aspects of her teaching on marriage. "It may be," he said, "that we have accentuated the Gospel text 'Increase and multiply' to such a point that we have obscured another text: 'and they will be two in one flesh.' "[43] He recommended cooperation between the Council and the papal birth control commission, and pointed out that there was much to learn from modern science. "We have made progress," he said, "since Aristotle [and even since Augustine] . . . I beg you, my brother bishops, let us avoid a new Galileo case. One is enough for the Church."[44] The need of incorporating new knowledge from contemporary science into the Church's teaching was urgent, he insisted, because thousands of the faithful were trying with anguish "to live in double fidelity, to the doctrine of the Church and to the demands of conjugal and parental love."[45]

Patriarch Maximos IV Saigh of Syria, the next speaker after Cardinal Suenens, gave what was perhaps the most revolutionary and outspoken talk of all. He referred to the "agonizing and burdensome" problem of birth control as the great crisis of Catholic conscience.

There is a question here of a break between the official doctrine of the Church and the contrary practice of the immense majority of Christian couples. The authority of the Church has been called into question on a vast scale. The faithful find themselves forced to live in conflict with the law of the Church, far from the sacraments, in constant anguish, unable to find a viable solution between two contradictory imperatives: conscience and normal married life.[46]

The Council, he declared, had to find a practical solution for this problem of conscience. The official position of the Church needed to be reviewed in the light of modern theological, medical, psychological, and sociological science, with married couples invited to collaborate in such a study. The Patriarch suggested that certain positions of the Church may have resulted not only from outmoded ideas, but also from a "bachelor psychosis" on the part of those with no experience of marriage. The Council had to face and attempt honestly to answer the question: "Is the external biological rectitude of an act the only criterion of morality, independent of family life, of its moral, conjugal, and family climate, and of the grave imperatives of prudence which must be the basic rule of all our human activity?"[47]

On October 30 Cardinal Bernard J. Alfrink of Utrecht, Holland, added his support to the remarks of the previous day's speakers. He, too, referred to the anxieties and difficulties experienced by married couples in their efforts to respond generously to the demands of their vocation. In some cases these difficulties had threatened the basic human values in marriage; in other cases they had led to estrangement from the Church. Obviously, Cardinal Alfrink said, the Church as the guardian of the divine law could not resolve these difficulties by a repudiation of that law. At the same time she could not ignore the fact that new anthropological knowledge had raised serious questions, hitherto unasked, about the meaning of the divine law. Calling attention to the growing recognition of the essential distinction between mere biological sexuality and human sexuality, he said:

. . . an honest doubt is arising among many married people and also among scientists and some theologians regarding at least the arguments used to prove that the only efficacious moral and Christian solution to such conflicts in the married life of the faithful of good will is complete or periodic continence.[48]

The situation, he continued, was too serious to permit the Church to decide this real conflict hastily and prematurely. But the situation had to be faced: fidelity to the divine law must be combined with solicitude for human problems. "Only if there is really certainty regarding the knowledge of the true content of divine law can and must the Church bind or free the consciences of her faithful."[49]

NOTES

1. John J. Lynch, "Notes on Moral Theology," *Theological Studies* 26 (June, 1965), p. 267.

2. Thomas D. Roberts, statement in *Search* (April, 1964), quoted in Pyle, *The Pill and Birth Regulation*, p. 86.

3. *Op. cit.*, p. 90.

4. Maurice O'Leary, "Debate over Birth Control Clarified," *Catholic Herald*, April 24, 1964.

5. *Ibid.*

6. *Ibid.*

7. Auberon Waugh, *Catholic Herald*, May 1, 1964.

8. "Bishops' Statement," *Catholic Herald*, May 8, 1964.

9. Richard A. Pring, Letter to the Editor, *Catholic Herald*, May 1, 1964.

10. P. Glazebrook, *Search* (June, 1964), quoted in Pyle, *op. cit.*, p. 106.

11. Norman St. John-Stevas, "Catholics and Birth Control," *The Observer*, May 3, 1964, quoted in Pyle, *op. cit.*, p. 108.

12. W. J. Reilly, Letter to the Editor, *London Tablet*, May 9, 1964.

13. Letter to the Editor, *Catholic Herald*, June 26, 1964.

14. Alfredo Ottaviani, *Vita*, quoted in *Catholic Herald*, May 29, 1964.

15. Paul VI, *Acta Apostolicae Sedis*, July 31, 1964.

16. John J. Lynch, "Notes on Moral Theology," *Theological Studies* 27 (June, 1966), p. 257.

17. *Ibid.*

18. Gerald Kelly, "Contraception and Natural Law," *Proceedings of the Catholic Theological Society* (June, 1963), p. 27.

19. Gerald Kelly, "Notes on Moral Theology," *Theological Studies* 24 (December, 1963), p. 635.

20. *Op. cit.*, p. 637.

21. Germain G. Grisez, *Contraception and the Natural Law* (Milwaukee: Bruce Publishing Co., 1964), p. 20 *et. seq.*

22. *Op. cit.*, p. 62.

23. *Op. cit.*, p. 92.

24. *Ibid.*

25. Louis Dupré, "A Critique of the Argument against Contraception Presented by Grisez," *National Catholic Reporter*, April 28, 1965.

26. *Ibid.*

27. *Ibid.*

28. Louis Dupré, "From Augustine to Janssens," *Commonweal* 80 (June 5, 1964), pp. 336–342.

29. Louis Dupré, "Toward a Reexamination of the Catholic Position on Birth Control," *Cross Currents* 14 (Winter, 1964), pp. 63–85. This article was actually written several months earlier than the article of Archbishop Roberts in *Search*.

30. Louis Dupré, *Contraception and Catholics* (Baltimore: Helicon Press, Inc., 1964), p. 40.

31. Dupré, *Contraception and Catholics*, p. 44.

32. Dupré, *Contraception and Catholics*, p. 78.

33. Gregory Baum, "Can the Church Change Her Position on Birth Control?" in Roberts, *Contraception and Holiness*, p. 344.

34. Michael Novak, ed., *The Experience of Marriage* (New York: The Macmillan Company, 1964), pp. xvii–173.

35. William Birmingham, *What Modern Catholics Think about Birth Control* (Signet Books. New York: New American Library, 1964).

36. *Op. cit.*, p. 113.

37. *Op. cit.*, pp. 28–73.

38. It is no reflection on the value of Daniel Sullivan's essay to say that a much more detailed and authoritative treatment of the history of contraception in the Catholic Church can be found in the truly monumental work published in 1965 by John T. Noonan, Jr., a professor of law at Notre Dame Law School. Noonan's Book, *Contraception: A History of Its Treatment by Catholic Theologians and Canonists,* is a thorough scholarly, objective analysis of the growth of the Church's doctrine from the first century to the present. It discusses the various historical and cultural forces which shaped that doctrine and shows the potentialities of that doctrine for further development. This is a work which will unquestionably remain for a long time the definitive historical study of its subject.

39. Birmingham, *op. cit.*, p. 15.

40. Paul-Emile Leger, *National Catholic Reporter*, November 11, 1964.

41. *Ibid.*

42. *Ibid.*

43. Leo Suenens, *National Catholic Reporter*, November 11, 1964.

44. *Ibid.*

45. *Ibid.*

46. Patriarch Maximos IV Saigh, *National Catholic Reporter*, November 11, 1964.

47. *Ibid.*

48. Bernard J. Alfrink, *National Catholic Reporter*, November 11, 1964.

49. *Ibid.*

VII THE PAPAL COMMISSION ON BIRTH CONTROL

On June 3, 1963, Pope John XXIII died, mourned by a world that had come to love him. In bequeathing to the Church a new spirit of openness to the world, he had left to his successor a great deal of unfinished business. Most important of that unfinished business was, of course, the Second Vatican Council which Pope John had convened and guided through its initial session. Another pending matter was that of the Pontifical Study Commission on Family Population and Birth Problems, whose original purpose, apparently, had been to examine the policies of the United Nations on the population question and to recommend to the Holy See the course of action that the Church should pursue in the light of these policies and of her own teaching on the subject of birth regulation. At the time of John's death, this papal study group—which had yet to hold its first meeting —scarcely seemed deserving of mention.

THE FIRST THREE SESSIONS

The first meeting of the commission was held at Louvain in the fall of 1963. At the time it was a small group composed of six members and a chairman. The chairman was a Swiss Dominican, Rev. Henri de Riedmatten, a "career diplomat" of the Vatican, who may have initially suggested the commission to Pope John. The other members were a French Jesuit, Stanislas de Lestapis; an English physician, John Marshall; an American population expert, Dr. Thomas Burch; a German moral theologian, Joseph Fuchs, S.J.; and Canon Pierre de Locht and Dr. P. van Rossum, both of Brussels.

Following this initial exploratory meeting, the decision was made to enlarge the group and make it more representative. It had become apparent that there was need for a broader inquiry not only into the policies of the United Nations but, because of recent controversies within the Church, into the Church's own teaching on birth regulation. The commission, enlarged to at least thirteen members,[1] convened in a second session in Rome during Easter Week of 1964; it was instructed to give priority in its deliberations to a study of the moral and doctrinal aspects of the problem of birth control.

A third session was planned for September, 1964, but late in May the commission members were quite suddenly summoned to Rome. At this meeting they were asked to give immediate attention to certain matters. In particular, Pope Paul VI wanted their advice on the morality of the pill, as he intended to make a firm statement on birth control when he addressed the cardinals in June.

The members of the commission were lodged at the Domus Maria on the via Aurelia. The meeting lasted five days, with sessions beginning at eight-thirty in the morning and concluding at five o'clock in the afternoon, but the commission was not able to arrive at any definitive conclusion. "Approximately two-thirds of the commission opposed the pill; almost half thought it was not opportune for the Pope to make a statement."[2]

Because of the inconclusiveness of the commission's deliberations, Pope Paul did not issue the firm statement on birth control that he had hoped to make. Instead, as we have seen earlier, in his address to the cardinals on June 23 he simply announced the existence of the commission, and indicated that he looked forward to a speedy conclusion of its work because "We hope soon to say our word supported by the light of human science."[3]

THE FOURTH SESSION

After this third session of the commission, Pope Paul decided once again to enlarge the group. For several months during the summer and fall of 1964, discreet and worldwide investigation was made to find qualified persons, and a number received letters of appointment on November 20, 1964. The letter, from Cardinal Amleto Giovanni Cicognani, the papal secretary of state, informed each new member: "The Holy Father has deigned to appoint you a member of the special committee for studies on problems of population and birth control."

By the end of 1964 the commission totaled fifty-eight members, among whom were three married couples and five lay women.[4] The chairman was Archbishop Leo Binz of St. Paul, Minnesota; the general secretary, Father de Riedmatten. The group was truly international; members came from every continent and from approximately twenty countries. There were representatives of current thought in moral theology, medicine and psychology; experts in research and practical involvement as well in the fields of demography, economics, sociology, and pastoral work in preparing people for marriage. For the first time the lay members of the group outnumbered the clergy.

Though the appointments to the commission had been made before the end of 1964, the members were not called together till late March, 1965. During this interval a provisional executive committee, under the leadership of Father de Riedmatten, met twice in Brussels —once on December 6, 1964, and again on March 6-7, 1965,—to arrange the agenda for the fourth session. De Riedmatten kept in touch with the commission members by mail. He requested that they prepare papers on specific topics in their own area of competency for discussion at the general meeting. He also sent each a questionnaire which covered twelve topics that would be taken up at the March meeting with a view to recommending some immediate practical course of action to the Holy See.

The fourth session was held in Rome from March 25 to 28, at the Pontificio Collegio Spagnolo on the via Torre Rossa. The Spanish College had only recently been constructed as a residence for Spanish theological students and had not yet been officially opened. Its choice as a meeting place was apparently dictated by the desire to keep the deliberations of the commission and even the fact of its meeting as secret as possible. For four days and nights the male members of the commission remained within the confines of the Collegio Spagnolo; the five women left each evening for the nearby convent of the Institute Mater Immaculata on the via Monte Gallo, where they were lodged for the night.

The daily schedule of meetings was a rigorous one. Mass was celebrated at 7:30 A.M. Following breakfast, the formal discussions began at 9 A.M. and lasted until 7:30 P.M. Dinner was at eight, after which all the commissioners met to listen to a talk on some topic pertinent to their discussions. The day's session terminated at 10 P.M. when the doors of the Collegio were locked. (One evening several of the men "escaped" from the Collegio for a brief period of relaxation at a sidewalk cafe, after having "bribed" the porter to leave the door open till eleven o'clock.)[5]

Each commission member was assigned, according to his own field of specialization, to one of three sectional groups: (1) the theological section, (2) the section on medicine and psychology, or (3) the section on demography, economics and sociology. The meetings of the different sections were so arranged that the commissioners were usually able to attend the sessions of their own group and to sit in on the meetings of the other sections as well. According to the procedural rules, at a particular sectional meeting only those who belonged to that section could ask "live" questions on the topic under discussion; other commission members, however, were allowed to present questions in writing.

During the four-day session the theological section, under the chairmanship of Rev. Jan Visser, held eight meetings; the section on medicine and psychology, directed by Dr. John Marshall and Dr.

J. R. Bertolus, respectively, held six; the one on demography, economics and sociology, presided over by Prof. Colin Clark of England, held five.

The Debate on Immediate Action

Since the purpose of the four-day session was not simply to study various aspects of the birth control problem, but to make specific recommendations to the Pope concerning the immediate course of action, the commission members, from the very start, were conscious of the special importance attached to the two Saturday afternoon meetings at which they would discuss in a plenary session what these recommendations would be. Indeed, the commission members had been prepared for this discussion even before the meeting was convened, for each had received from the general secretary a twelve-point questionnaire detailing the subjects that would be brought up in the "debate on immediate action."

The questionnaire was comprehensive. It pointed to four areas of basic importance in the theology of marriage—responsibility in parenthood, the importance of conjugal love, the significance of sexuality in marriage, the need for education—and posed the question: Did the members of the commission feel that sufficiently significant doctrinal progress had been made for a pronouncement by the Church on these matters? The questionnaire also brought up the problem of methods of birth regulation. Should there be a pronouncement encouraging wider use of periodic continence? Should similar encouragement be given to certain legitimate uses of the pill? Were some methods of birth regulation already condemned by the magisterium intrinsically evil and, if so, should a reminder be issued making it clear that these methods were still condemned?

Still other questions concerned the Church's teaching and the possibility of change in that teaching. If a pronouncement were to be made modifying some aspects of the Church's teaching, how would the commissioners suggest that this change be presented: as a repudiation of past reformable teaching, or as a development of doctrine in the light of new facts? Or if it were decided that no pronouncement should be made at the present time, what practical advice could be given to priests and confessors as guides for pastoral counseling in particular cases?

The final question in the questionnaire went beyond the birth control controversy. It asked whether or not the divergent opinions on the moral issues involved in that controversy were rooted in fundamentally different doctrinal positions that affected much wider areas of theology than the specific subject under discussion in the commission.

Unfortunately the time allotted for "the debate on immediate action" was insufficient for a discussion of all the points contained in the questionnaire. A number of significant points of accord emerged, however. There was general agreement that the teaching on marriage which the world was expecting from the Church required further maturing and more detailed study before it could be presented in its entirety. But there was also general agreement on the desirability of an immediate pronouncement from the Pope that would take the form of a basic document on marriage. The commission members believed that the document should stress the importance of responsible parenthood, the place of conjugal love and human sexuality in marriage, and the need for extensive education of children, adolescents, engaged couples, and married people in the Christian teaching on marriage. Such a pronouncement, it was felt, would help to clarify the present situation and offer basic guidelines that would facilitate the future research of theologians and specialists in other fields.

The majority of the commission favored the encouragement of a wider use of periodic continence, though some pointed out that it should by no means be presented as a solution to every problem. Others (notably Mr. and Mrs. Patrick Crowley of Chicago, who had conducted an extensive survey among C.F.M. couples) warned that in many cases the use of rhythm created more problems than it solved.

There was no general agreement on the pill. Some proposed immediate approval of its use in cases of necessity. Others felt that a pronouncement at that time would be inopportune. A minority asked for condemnation of the pill except in those cases already approved by theologians. As for reiterating any past condemnations, the majority of the commission took the position that it was not then advisable.

Most of the members of the commission shared a common sense of urgency. Their work must continue. There was need to act as quickly as possible in all areas that needed further clarification.

AUDIENCE WITH THE POPE

On March 27, 1965, the entire commission was received in audience by Pope Paul VI. In his remarks, delivered in French, the Pope expressed his gratitude for the "earnestness" with which they had accepted the responsibility he had placed upon them to assist the Church in answering, with the help of contemporary science and in the light of faith, the question: "In what form and according to what norms must married couples fulfill, in the exercise of their mutual love, this service of life to which they are called by their vocation?"[6]

Twice in the course of his talk he echoed the sentiments of the commission when he stressed the urgency of the problem that had brought them together. The first time was when he said:

The conscience of men cannot be left exposed to the uncertainties which too often today prevent conjugal life from developing according to the design of God. Furthermore, beyond the very urgent questions of married couples, there are economic and social problems which, as we said in our allocution of June 23 [1964], the Church cannot ignore.[7]

And, toward the end of his talk: "The question is too important, the uncertainties of some persons are too painful for you not to feel driven by a sense of urgency, which is that of charity toward all those to whom we owe an answer."[8]

At the same time, the Pope acknowledged that the complexity of the problem and the several levels of knowledge at which their research had to be carried out might necessitate "reasonable delays." He asked the members of the commission to examine the question "in all serenity and liberty of spirit," allowing that to mature which must mature, and working diligently, without concern about criticism and difficulties, in the realization that they were acting in the service of the Church and of the Vicar of Christ.

Conclusion of the Meeting

At the close of the fourth session of the papal commission on birth control, the members, preparing to leave Rome, had various reactions as they looked back on their four-days' meeting. They were all too conscious of the fact that many questions were still unresolved and that much work remained to be done. They were aware too of the difficulties they had faced and only partially surmounted. There had been too many papers and too little time for discussion; the translation facilities had been notoriously poor.

Nevertheless there was a sense of accomplishment; much had been done, particularly within the commission itself. A group which in the beginning had been largely strangers to one another, had come together for four days of talk, study, and discussion and had emerged with a strong sense of community and brotherly feeling. They had worked harmoniously together, learning from one another and being enriched by the vast fund of knowledge they had been able to share.

The constant demand on the part of the lay members for greater clarity had opened new and hitherto unseen perspectives for the theologians. The contribution of the married couples had been especially important. At times it appeared to them that the theologians were speaking about marriage in a language far removed from the reality that they knew from experience. Once, in a moment of exasperation, one of the married women had been heard to murmur: "But we are talking about us!"

The members of the commission departed from the Collegio Spagnolo with an urgent dedication to the work that still remained to be done. A small group[9] remained an extra day to assist Henri de Riedmatten in preparing a report of the meeting. This report, summarizing the conclusions and recommendations of the commission, was written on Monday, March 29, and submitted by Father de Riedmatten to the Pope.

SESSION 4 OF VATICAN II

In addition to preparing a report for the Pope, some members of the commission's executive committee met in April, 1965, with the Conciliar Commission, which was engaged in rewriting the draft of Schema 13, to offer recommendations for that part of the schema (Chapter 1 of Part II) that dealt with marriage and the family.

The revised draft, incorporating the suggestions made by the bishops at the previous session of the Council with the recommendations of the papal commission on birth control, was presented to the bishops in the fall of 1965. In a preliminary vote,[10] taken in November, 1965, the schema was adopted by an overwhelming majority. The document was then referred back to the "mixed commission,"[11] which had drawn up the schema. According to the procedural rules under which the Council operated, each amendment to the text, as suggested by the bishops, had to be considered and a decision made as to which of them could be properly incorporated into the document. The amendments proposed for Chapter 1 of Part II were turned over to a subcommittee of the mixed commission, whose chairman was Archbishop John F. Dearden of Detroit.

THE PAPAL *MODI* AND FOOTNOTE 14

On November 24, 1965, the mixed commission met to consider the final draft of Chapter 1, Part II, as it had been prepared by Archbishop Dearden's subcommittee. At the beginning of the meeting the chairman, Cardinal Ottaviani, called upon the secretary, Father Sebastian Tromp, to read an important communication. This was a letter from Cardinal Cicognani, the papal secretary of state, proposing, "in the name of a higher authority," four amendments (*modi*) to be introduced into the text. It was quite clear that "the higher authority" was Pope Paul VI. It was equally clear that the intent of the *modi* was to reassert in the document two elements of the traditional teaching on marriage: (1) the hierarchy of ends in marriage, and (2) the condemnation of contraception.

The letter caused great consternation among the majority of commission members. The text already approved by the Council had carefully avoided the distinction between the primary and secondary ends of marriage; its introduction, therefore, would mean a substantial modification of the text. Furthermore, since the topic of contraception had been removed from the agenda of the Council by the Pope himself, the inclusion in any form of an explicit condemnation of contraception would force the Council to take a stand on an issue that it had not been permitted to discuss.

Xavier Rynne wrote that not all at the meeting were dismayed by the communication:

When the *modi* were read, to the consternation of the subcommission members, there was a look of triumph on the faces of the American Jesuit Father John Ford and the Franciscan Father Ermenegildo Lio, advocates of an intransigent position on the subject of birth control, while Cardinal Browne is alleged to have said, "*Christus ipse locutus est*—Christ Himself has spoken."[12]

The commission requested a clarification, and on November 26 received a second letter from Cardinal Cicognani. This letter insisted that the papal *modi* be incorporated into the document, though their exact wording could be left to the discretion of the commission. With this leeway, the commission, after much debate, was able to modify the text without drastically altering it.

The second of the four *modi* called for an addition to Article 50. Unmodified, the addition would have amounted to an affirmation of the distinction between primary and secondary ends of marriage. The commission managed to reword the article so that the emphasis on procreation required by the papal *modus* was expressed in such a way as to not prejudice the other ends of marriage. The reworded article said, in effect, that the fecundity with which God blesses marriage is a great gift to parents, but it does not put the other ends of marriage in second place.[13] The commission, therefore, refused to commit the Council document to a reaffirmation of the traditional notion of an hierarchy of ends in marriage.

Of the other three *modi,* the first and the third were especially important, for their evident intent was to incorporate into the Council document the traditional condemnation of contraception as affirmed by Pius XI in *Casti Connubii.* Modus I proposed an addition to Article 47, which listed the various ills that threaten modern marriage: polygamy, divorce, the worship of pleasure, etc. The papal *modus* proposed adding "contraceptive practices" (*artes anticonceptionales*) to this list, with a footnote reference to *Casti Connubii.*[14] The commission, after some discussion, added instead the more general phrase, "illicit practices against human generation" (*usus illicitus contra generationem*). It did not specify what these illicit practices were. The reference to *Casti Connubii* was omitted.

Modus III called for an addition to Article 51, which originally stated that Catholics may not use methods of birth regulation proscribed by the teaching authority of the Church. The *modus* proposed that the wording be changed to read "methods of birth regulation which have been or will be proscribed (*improbatae sunt vel improbentur*) by the teaching authority of the Church." In addition the *modus* required that there be appended to the words "have been proscribed" (*improbatae sunt*) a footnote citing *Casti Connubii* and Pius XII's allocution to the Italian midwives. Since this *modus* involved a clear reaffirmation of the teaching of *Casti Connubii* on contraception and the confirmation of that teaching in Pius XII's allocution, acceptance of it—besides putting the Council on record as having given a definitive answer to an undiscussed question—would have made the work of the papal commission on birth control superfluous.

After some discussion, the commission decided to substitute the present tense of the verb for the past and future tenses recommended by the *modus*. The new reading was little more than a variation of the original text; it simply said that Catholics must not use "methods of birth regulation which are proscribed by the teaching authority of the Church." The footnote (No. 14 in the Latin text) was appended as the modus had requested, but in addition to citing *Casti Connubii* and Pius XII's allocution to the Italian midwives, it included a reference to Pope Paul's June, 1964, announcement to the cardinals of the creation of the papal commission to study the problem of birth control. The inclusion of this third reference in the footnote made it possible to see a development in the Church's teaching, with each of the three documents representing a stage in that development. The commission also attached to the footnote a statement asserting that the Council did not intend to propose any concrete solutions to the birth control problem because the question was being studied by a special papal commission.

Pope Paul unhesitatingly accepted the modification made by the commission. Thus, despite behind-the-scenes pressure brought to bear by the conservative element in the Curia, the mixed commission was able to preserve intact the original meaning of the document approved by the Council. The document did not reaffirm the hierarchy of ends in marriage; it remained uncommitted on specific questions about birth regulation, leaving these to be dealt with by the special commission set up by the Pope.

THE FIFTH SESSION OF THE PONTIFICAL STUDY COMMISSION ON FAMILY, POPULATION AND BIRTH PROBLEMS

The fifth and final session of the papal commission on birth control was held in Rome in the spring of 1966. This meeting differed in a number of respects from the meeting of the previous year. First of all, the commission itself had been reorganized; in February, 1966, Pope Paul had named sixteen bishops, including seven cardinals, to act as an executive committee.[15] This meant that the commission, instead of being advisors directly responsible to the Pope, became advisors (*periti*) to the committee of bishops who, in their turn, were to report to the Pope.

Another significant difference was the length of time allotted to the meeting. The 1965 meeting had lasted only four days; the fifth session met for more than two months—from April 18 to June 28—though not all of the commission members were present for the entire time. The lengthening of the session made it possible to organize the meeting along different lines. Each section had time to hold meetings of its own that lasted for several days; moreover, a new section was added to the three already existing—a pastoral section. This new section, which held two week-long meetings (May 9–14 and June 6–10), was made up of the theological section and representatives from the other two sections.[16] Since it represented all three of the original groups, the pastoral section was something of a miniature version of the entire commission; its deliberations and conclusions, therefore, proved to be especially significant.

It was not only in organization and scheduling that the fifth session differed from the previous one. The spirit and atmosphere were also different. Men and women who had come to the Collegio Spagnolo the year before as strangers returned there as friends. The sense of community and brotherhood that they had experienced in the previous session made possible a much freer and more open dialogue. But perhaps the most meaningful change was a much sharper definition of purpose. As the members of the commission continued to work together, it became more and more evident that there was one crucial issue which they had to face—not rhythm or the pill, but the issue of contraception. The discussions converged more and more on two different but closely related questions: (1) Was contraception intrinsically evil? (2) Was it possible for the Church to change her teaching on contraception?

It is probably true to say that at the time of their appointments most of the commissioners, however varied their opinions may have been on the use of rhythm or the pill, were convinced that contraception was immoral and that no fundamental revision of the Church's position was possible. But as they studied and discussed the traditional theological arguments against contraception, they began to see that the arguments were not nearly so convincing as they had once thought. Many—indeed, the great majority—experienced a radical change in thinking and reached the conclusion that the intrinsic evil of contraception could not be convincingly demonstrated by reasoning based on natural law. One commissioner admitted that he formerly had no doubts that the teaching of the Church was correct and that artificial birth control was intrinsically evil. "I no longer feel that way," he said.

When I ask myself why I changed, it seems that up to three years ago I accepted this teaching without question. Now having studied it, I find it is no longer acceptable. I am in no position to discuss the theological aspects of the problem. The position taken by the majority of the theologians on the commission is very convincing. I would tend to disregard the few negative opinions, because they are held by very rigid individuals in whom change is unlikely.[17]

Even Father John Ford, whose intransigent stand on the immorality of contraception would have led many to classify him among the "very rigid" members of the commission, acknowledged the inconclusiveness of the natural law argument. In a paper prepared for the third session of the commission, Father Ford had stated: "We lack convincing arguments from natural law which are universally valid and universally admitted."[18] In the same paper he conceded: "Unfortunately in the case of contraception and contraceptive sterilization the theologians have not, up to now, produced arguments which are clear, convincing, universally valid and admitted by all."[19]

For Father Ford, however, the decisive factor in the discussion of contraception was not the inconclusiveness of the natural law argument, but the authority of the Church. The Church has taught that contraception is immoral because it violates the natural law. It was Father Ford's opinion that just as the Church, in defining a dogma as revealed, is not obliged to indicate the particular places in Scripture and tradition where this dogma may be found, neither is She obliged, in defining a moral doctrine, to point out the precise reasoning which demonstrates that doctrine. This, he felt, was a task for the theologians. The fact that the theologians had thus far been unsuccessful in accomplishing this task with regard to contraception did not foreshadow a change in the Church's teaching; rather it offered a challenge to the theologians to discover better and more cogent reasons for more effectively defending the Church's position.

Not many of the commissioners were disposed to follow Father Ford's line of reasoning. In fact, as the session progressed and the radical revisionists became aware of the numerical strength of their position, the movement for change gathered so much momentum that Father Ford complained: "Since all the sessions were conducted with the implicit assumption that the Church will change her position, the opportunity for meaningful participation by those who believe that radical revision is impossible was considerably decreased."[20]

TWO WORKING PAPERS

Toward the end of May the two positions that had come into focus at the sessions were given expression in two working papers, one produced by the "conservative" minority ("The State of the Question: the Doctrine of the Church and Its Authority") and the other by the "liberal" majority ("Summary Document on the Morality of Birth Control").[21]

The minority paper, drawn up by John Ford and signed by three other theologians (Visser, Zalba and de Lestapis), viewed the contraceptive issue from a perspective that was primarily ecclesiological. It argued that the Church had already answered the question: Is contraception always seriously evil? Her answer, unequivocally affirmative, could be found in *Casti Connubii,* the 1951 and 1958 allocutions of Pius XII, *Mater et Magistra* of Pope John XXIII, and in numerous statements of national hierarchies and individual bishops. "One can find no period of history, no document of the Church, no theological school, scarcely one Catholic theologian who ever denied that contraception was always seriously evil. The teaching of the Church in this matter is absolutely constant."[22]

It was impossible, the minority paper insisted, for the Church to change her answer to this question "because this answer is true";[23] and it must be true because the Church, instituted by Christ to lead men to salvation "could not have erred through so many centuries, even through one century, by imposing under serious obligation very grave burdens in the name of Jesus Christ, if Jesus Christ did not actually impose these burdens."[24]

To say that the Church had erred in this one matter would be to call into question the authority of the ordinary magisterium in all moral matters. It would, moreover, imply that in 1930, 1951, and 1958 the Holy Spirit had assisted the Protestant churches and allowed the Catholic Church to condemn under pain of eternal damnation thousands upon thousands of human acts that really were not sinful.

While admitting that the natural law arguments prohibiting contraception were not always plain and compelling, the minority paper argued that one fact, at least, was clear: The Church has always taught the inviolability of the generative process. This inviolability is analogous to the inviolability of human life itself; and just as human life is removed from the dominion of man, so also are the sources of life.

The authors of the minority paper also placed great stress on the evil consequences that would result if contraception were allowed. They argued that the reasons used to justify contraception could also be used to justify evils such as extramarital relations, perverse sexual acts in marriage, masturbation and direct sterilization. Giving approval to contraception, therefore, would not only undermine the teaching authority of the Church, it would also call into question the essentially unchangeable character of the natural law.

The majority paper, prepared by Joseph Fuchs, Philip Delhaye and Raymond Sigmund, viewed the question of intervention in intercourse from a totally different standpoint than the minority statement. It saw the official teaching of the Church in the process of evolution from *Casti Connubii,* through the teachings of Pius XII and, finally, in the teachings of Vatican II. *Casti Connubii* was admittedly of special importance, yet it had to be seen in its historical setting; the encyclical simply reaffirmed the common teaching of most Christians at the time. "The solemnity of the condemnation of every contraceptive intervention is especially understandable as a reaction to the declaration of the Lambeth Conference."[25]

The tradition which *Casti Connubii* affirmed, however, was not apostolic nor could it be demonstrated from Scripture. Expressed in different ways at different times, it represented the Church's constant concern for the goodness of procreation, in opposition to the Gnostics, the Manichaeans and later the Cathari, all of whom asserted that procreation was evil.

The arguments which *Casti Connubii* adduced against contraceptive intervention were vague and imprecise because they were based on an inadequate concept of natural law developed over the past three centuries. This concept did not sufficiently take into account the fact that man, as God's creature, is "the prudent administrator and steward of the gifts of nature." It looked upon the gifts of nature as an immediate expression of God's will, ignoring the fact that man is called by God to take command of nature and to shape it to worthy human purposes. "Churchmen," the majority paper asserted, "have been slower than the rest of the world in clearly seeing this as man's vocation."[26]

The majority paper faced head-on the two main arguments of the conservative statement. In reply to the ecclesiological argument, it stated that "the criteria for discerning what the Spirit could or could not permit in the Church can scarcely be determined *a priori*."[27] It further indicated that in recent decades there had been an unfortunate tendency to obscure the distinction between non-infallible teachings of the Church and those that are infallible; thus, the first were considered as unreformable as the second. This was not good theology, since a teaching that is non-infallible is by that very fact open to the possibility of reform. It was not good history, either, for there have been times when the magisterium has been in error as, for example, when the Church, with the active concurrence of the popes, taught for many centuries that intercourse without the explicit intention of procreation was illicit—a position that no one in the Church would hold today.

To admit that such mistakes have been made in the past would not undermine the confidence of Catholics in the teaching authority of the Church, nor would it mean that other teachings would be called into question. Change in a teaching comes about not simply because the teaching is non-infallible but because there is some reason for change; consequently, changes would not be contemplated in areas where no such reasons exist. As the majority paper put it: "Doubt and reconsideration are quite reasonable when proper reasons for doubt and reconsideration occur with regard to some specific question. This is part and parcel of the accepted teaching of fundamental theology."[28]

The conservative argument concerning the inviolability of the generative process was also rejected by the majority paper as an erroneous understanding of nature. Such an unconditional respect for nature as it is in itself ignored the fact that the dominion of God is exercised through man who, in liberty and responsibility, is called by God to use nature for his own perfection according to the dictates of right reason. "The order of creation does not require that all things be left untouchable just as they are, but that they reach the ends to which they have been ordered."[29] When man uses his skill to intervene in the biological processes of nature, the morality of such intervention depends on whether or not it accords with right reason. Intercourse has a material orientation toward fecundity, but this must be rationally directed by man. "Finalization toward fecundity can formally come only from man, though this finality is found materially in the organs."[30]

Stressing the fact that intervention in intercourse must be seen in the context of responsible parenthood, the majority paper stated:

When man intervenes in the procreative process, he does this with the intention of regulating and not excluding fertility. Then he unites the material finality toward fecundity which exists in intercourse with the formal finality of the person and renders the entire process "human."[31]

In other words, marriage, but not necessarily every conjugal act, must be open to life, for such acts which are infertile by intention or rendered infertile by intervention are ordered to the expression of a couple's union in love. Infertile conjugal acts, therefore, cannot be judged moral or immoral in isolation from the total context of the marriage union; rather they derive their full moral quality from the fact that they are ordered to the fertility of the marriage relation as such.

Such an understanding of intervention in intercourse protects the good of procreation that was so strongly emphasized in *Casti Connubii* and in the tradition of the Church; but it protects it as a human good, not merely as a biological one.

THE REPORT OF THE
THEOLOGICAL SECTION

The April 19, 1967, issue of the *National Catholic Reporter* published three documents of the papal commission on birth control. The first two, just discussed, were working papers, composed primarily for use within the commission to clarify the two divergent positions that had emerged from the deliberations. The third document, "An Outline for a Document on Responsible Parenthood," was of much greater importance. Written by six members of the theological section,[32] it was intended as an official report from the commission to Pope Paul VI. Dated May 26, 1966, it was discussed and given its final wording at the final week's session of the pastoral section (June 6–10). It represented the mature fruits of several years of study and deliberation and was approved by a large majority of the commission.[33] On June 23 it was presented to the bishops.

Though drawn up by the same theologians, the report was markedly different in tone from the majority paper. The majority paper had been written in rebuttal to the arguments of the conservative position; it was, therefore, frankly polemic in character. This third document was much more positive and doctrinal in its approach. Apparently intended to serve as the basis for a papal statement that would settle the birth control problem in the Church, it attempted to treat the problem in the context of a contemporary theology of marriage.

Drawing liberally on the teaching of Vatican II, the report presented marriage as a community of persons, rooted in conjugal love and made fruitful by the creation of new human life. It recognized that only in the context of truly responsible parenthood could the basic values of conjugal love and marital fecundity be integrated so that one is not sacrificed to the other. It acknowledged further that for most married couples responsible parenthood requires a prudent and reasonable regulation of conception. "If they are to observe and cultivate all the essential values of marriage, married people need decent and human means for the regulation of conception."[34]

The moral rectitude of these means did not require the direct fecundity of each and every particular act of intercourse. It did require that these means be directed to the fecundity of marriage as a whole. Responsible parenthood, therefore, would exclude a contraceptive mentality that would "egoistically and irrationally" oppose fruitfulness; it would not exclude intervention in intercourse that is ordered to a fruitful married life.

The theologians were especially concerned about showing that the doctrine which they propounded represented a continuity of the essential elements of the tradition which the Church had taught in the past. Indeed, the report stated, values affirmed in that tradition were better safeguarded in the new teaching than in the old:

The true opposition is not to be sought between some material conformity to the physiological processes of nature and some artificial intervention. For it is natural to man to use his skill in order to put under human control what is given by physical nature. The opposition is really to be sought between one way of acting which is contraceptive and opposed to prudent and generous fruitfulness, and another way which is in an ordered relationship to responsible fruitfulness and which has a concern for education and all the essential human and Christian values. In such a concept the substance of tradition stands in continuity and is respected. . . . The moral obligation of following fundamental norms and fostering all the essential values in a balanced fashion is strengthened and not weakened.[35]

THE VOTING ON THE THEOLOGIANS' REPORT

After the bishops received the report on June 23, they amended it in several respects and then voted on its acceptance. Of the fifteen bishops in attendance, nine voted in favor of it, three were against it, and three were doubtful.[36]

It is interesting to note that this vote was taken exactly two years from the date (June 23, 1964) on which Pope Paul had announced to the cardinals the formation of the commission.

The Voting on Contraception

The following day the bishops met in a morning session in which they discussed three questions, the most crucial of which was the one that had dominated the fifth session of the commission: Is contraception intrinsically evil? The other two questions were corollaries of this: the one concerned the means of contraception; the other, the wisdom of a public pronouncement on birth control by the magisterium.

After an hour's deliberation, a written vote was taken. The voting on the question, Is contraception intrinsically evil? was as follows: yes, 2; yes, with reservations 1; abstained 3; no 9.

A substantial majority of the bishops, therefore, joined the very large majority of the commission members in asserting that contraception was not evil in itself. The significance of the voting by both groups was obvious. The papal commission on birth control had come to the conclusion that there now existed what Pope Paul had said did not exist in 1964—sufficient reason for modifying the Church's official teaching on birth control.

THE PASTORAL INTRODUCTION

Yet a fourth document was drawn up in the final days of this fifth session. This document grew out of a concern expressed by several bishops that the language of the theologians' report was too technical for the majority of the faithful. It was decided, therefore, to preface the report with a "pastoral introduction." The drafting of this document was entrusted to Bishop Claude Dupuy of Albi, France, the chairman of the pastoral section; the actual writing was done by a small group composed mainly of laymen from the same section.[37]

"Pastoral Approaches," as the document was called, covered much the same ground as that of the theologians' report. Though in briefer form, the language was less technical and its style often movingly impressive. It called attention to the evolution that had taken place in the Church's teaching on marriage, but showed at the same time that this evolution, rather than abandoning traditional values, actually deepened them.

It placed on both husband and wife the task of deciding the means of birth regulation that are to be employed, "without drifting into arbitrary decisions, but always taking account of the objective criteria of morality. These criteria are in the first place those that relate to the totality of married life and sexuality."[38]

Particularly noteworthy was the emphasis placed on the "rich experience of the faithful" and the contribution it has made to the development of the Church's doctrine on marriage. The Church, the document said, listens to this experience, clarifies it and authenticates it. And thus, it concluded:

In response to the questioning of her children and, beyond them, of the whole world, this is the beautiful but demanding teaching worthy of a humanity redeemed by the blood of Christ . . . that the Church proposes to the people of today. Through this teaching, today as in the past, the Church, protected from error in proclaiming the values whose essence has been confided to her through the word of her well-beloved Head, wishes to promote the Christian advancement of the family.[39]

The Report to the Pope

"Pastoral Approaches" was discussed by the bishops on June 25 and 26 and given their approval. This and the report of the theologians, to which the document served as an introduction, became the two official reports presented to the Pope in the name of the entire commission. A vast amount of additional material—including summaries of the meetings of the individual sections and a dossier of the papers and reports presented by individual members of the commission— was also given to the Pope. To facilitate its study and evaluation, Father de Riedmatten, assisted by some of the commission members, prepared summaries of the summaries as well as a detailed index of all the materials, with references and cross references to all aspects of the many topics that had been discussed during the session.

The entire report comprised twelve large volumes. On June 28, 1966, these twelve volumes were presented to Pope Paul VI by Cardinal Julius Döpfner of Munich, and Father de Riedmatten. The papal commission had finished its task. Its members had done their work thoroughly and had, as the Pope had charged them, allowed to mature what must mature. In the light of the best scientific and theological knowledge, they had spoken their word. Now it remained for the Pope to speak his word, as he had promised. The world waited and the commission waited.

THE PAPAL ALLOCUTION
OF OCTOBER 29, 1966

On October 29, 1966, Pope Paul received in audience delegates of the Italian Society of Obstetrics and Gynecology. There was much expectation that he would take this occasion to speak his mind. He did—not to settle the birth control question, however, but to give direction to the discussion of the subject that was going on in the Church.

The Pope disassociated himself from those who claimed that the teaching of Vatican II in *Gaudium et Spes* had opened the way to a change in the Church's doctrine. The Council, he said, had brought out certain principles that were most useful for the "integration" of Catholic doctrine on marriage but these principles were not of a kind to change the "substantial elements of that doctrine."[40] In effect, he also disassociated himself from the conclusions of the birth control commission. While praising the commission for the "great work" it had done, he nonetheless stated that the conclusions it had presented to him "cannot be considered definitive, because of the fact that they carry grave implications . . . in the pastoral and social spheres, which cannot be isolated or set aside."[41]

Finally, Pope Paul disassociated himself from those theologians who, in increasing numbers, were maintaining that a state of doubt existed in the Church, and who therefore felt that the faithful should consider themselves free to make their own conscientious decisions on the matter of birth control. Recalling his discourse of June 23, 1964, he stated:

. . . the norm, until now taught by the Church, integrated by the wise instructions of the Council, demands faithful and generous observance. It cannot be considered not binding, as if the magisterium of the Church were in a state of doubt at the present time, whereas it is rather in a moment of study and reflection.[42]

The practical conclusion of the Pope's statement was that, despite the great work completed by the commission, there was need for "a supplementary study" which, he said:

We are resolutely undertaking . . . with great reverence for those who have already given it so much attention and tiring labor, but likewise with a sense of the obligation of our apostolic office. And this is the reason why our response has been delayed and why it must be deferred for some time yet.[43]

Disappointment in the Pope's remarks was great. Many had hoped for a statement that would clarify the Church's official position on the birth control issue; instead, his words seemed to make that position even more puzzling. What precisely did it mean to be in a moment of study and reflection, yet not in a state of doubt? Why, if there was no doubt about the Church's position, was there need for further study and reflection? If there was need for further study and reflection, how could it be said that the Church was not in a state of doubt?

Some interpreted what the Pope had said to mean that while speculative doubt remained regarding the morality of contraception (and hence further study was required), there was no doubt about the practical course of action that should be followed until this study was completed (the norms of the past were to be followed). Such a distinction might satisfy a theologian, but a letter to the editor of the *London Tablet* expressed the bafflement of many lay people. It said: "It reduces a mere layman to a state of—well, my Roget seems to offer a couple of dozen direct alternatives, but none of them, I regret to say, is either 'study' or 'reflection'."[44]

In view of the subsequent publication of the encyclical *Humanae Vitae,* one may perhaps wonder: Is it possible that when he spoke to the obstetricians and gynecologists in 1966 the Pope had already decided what he must eventually do, i.e., repeat the ban on contraception? Had he, however, needed more time to decide how to say what he was convinced had to be said? Were more study and reflection required, not for the purpose of arriving at a conclusion, but for finding more forceful reasons for supporting the conclusion which he had already reached? Had it been just such support which the Pope had expected from the papal commission? Perhaps this was what he had meant when he said in his 1964 address to the cardinals, "We hope soon to say our word, *supported by the light of human science*."[45] When that support was not forthcoming from the papal commission, he may have felt obliged to turn to other sources. Was this the reason why he found it necessary to make a "supplementary study" and defer his decision "for some time yet"?

NOTES

1. At the second session, in addition to the original members, the commission included: Bernardo Colombo (statistician from Venice); Bernard Häring (German Redemptorist and moral theologian); Clement Mertens (Jesuit from Louvain); Prof. Jacques Mertens de Wilmars (from Brussels); Jan Visser (Dutch Redemptorist), and Marcelino Zalba (Spanish Jesuit teaching at the Gregorian University in Rome).

2. Desmond O'Grady, "Pontifical Commission," *National Catholic Reporter,* March 24, 1965.

3. Paul VI, *Acta Apostolicae Sedis,* July 31, 1964.

4. For a list of the membership, see Appendix I.

5. Lois R. Chevalier, "The Secret Drama behind the Pope's Momentous Decision on Birth Control," *Ladies Home Journal* (March, 1966), p. 167.

6. Paul VI, "Address to the Birth Control Group," *National Catholic Reporter,* April 7, 1965.

7. *Ibid.*

8. *Ibid.*

9. The executive committee that met with de Riedmatten included: Jan Visser, André Hellegers, Albert Görres, Michel Dembélé and Colin Clark. Two other members of the executive committee, Clement Mertens and Jacques Mertens de Wilmars, were absent.

10. According to the procedural rules under which the Council operated, the documents of the Council had to be voted on at least twice by the bishops. First, there was a preliminary vote on the proposed document, in which the Council Fathers had three options: they could vote (1) *placet* (yes), (2) *non-placet* (no),

or (3) *placet iuxta modum* (yes, but with qualifications). Those who voted *placet iuxta modum* were required to submit the amendments or qualifications (*modi*) which they wished to have incorporated into the text.

If a majority of the bishops approved the document in this preliminary vote, the proposed amendments were sent back to the commission which had originally drafted the document. The commission, in turn, referred these amendments to one of its own subcommittees (drafting committees), each responsible for a particular section of the document. The drafting committee, in considering the amendments, followed two procedural rules: (1) The proposed amendments, in order to be incorporated into the text, had to be accepted by two-thirds of the committee. (2) No amendment could be accepted that conflicted with the substance of the text already approved by the Council.

Once the drafting committees had completed their work, the revised text was submitted to the entire commission for its approval. Upon acceptance of the revised text by the full commission, the document was then submitted to the bishops for their final vote. In this final vote no amendments to the text could be made. In voting, the bishops had only two options: (1) *placet,* or (2) *non-placet.*

11. The commission that drew up the revised draft of Schema 13 was called the "mixed commission" because it was made up of representatives of the Commission for the Apostolate of the Laity (headed by Cardinal Cento) and of the Theological Commission (headed by Cardinal Ottaviani).

12. Xavier Rynne, *The Fourth Session* (New York: Farrar, Straus & Co., Inc., 1966), pp. 211-212.

13. Gregory Baum, "Birth Control—What Happened?" *Commonweal* 83 (December 24, 1965), p. 371.

14. "*Artes anti-conceptionales*" were the very words used in *Casti Connubii* in the condemnation of contraception.

15. The sixteen bishops included: Cardinals Döpfner (Munich), Gracias (Bombay), Heenan (London), Lefebre (Bourges), Ottaviani (Rome), Sheehan (Baltimore), Suenens (Malines-Brussels); and Bishops Binz (St. Paul), Colombo (theologian to the Pope), Dearden (Detroit), Dupuy (Albi), Mendez (Venezuela), Morris (Cashel, Ireland), Reuss (Mainz), Wojtla (Cracow), Zoa (Cameroons).

Cardinal Ottaviani was chairmen of the Bishops' Committee; Cardinal Döpfner and Cardinal Heenan were vice-chairmen.

Archbishop (now Cardinal) Wojtla was unable to attend because he was denied a visa by the Polish government.

16. The members of the theological section were the following: Archbishop Binz, Bishop Reuss, Paul Anciaux, Alfons Auer, John C. Ford, Joseph Fuchs,

Tullo Goffi, Albert Görres, Bernard Häring, George A. Kelly, Michel Labourdette, Ferdinando Lambruschini, Louis Lebret, Stanislas de Lestapis, Pierre de Locht, André van Melsen, G. Perico, Jan Visser, Marcelino Zalba.

The representatives of the two other sections were: Donald Barrett, J. R. Bertolus, John R. Cavanagh, Mr. and Mrs. Patrick Crowley, André Hellegers, Mrs. J. F. Kulanday, J. Lopez-Ibor, J. Margeot, John Marshall, Henri Moins, Paul Moriguchi, Dr. and Mme. Laurent Potvin, R. Rabary, Dr. and Mme. Henri Rendu.

Archbishop Dupuy was chairman of the pastoral section; Dr. André Hellegers was secretary.

17. John R. Cavanagh, Letter to Cardinal Heenan (June 20, 1966).

18. John C. Ford, paper written for the third session of the commission.

19. *Ibid.*

20. Written observations of certain theologians on the meetings of the pastoral section held during the week of May 9–14.

21. These papers, though never officially released, were published by the *National Catholic Reporter* (April 19, 1967), together with a third document bearing the title: "Outline for a Document on Responsible Parenthood." This document, as will be indicated later, was the most important of the three. The three documents and other related items are included in Robert G. Hoyt, ed., *The Birth Control Debate* (Kansas City: National Catholic Reporter, 1968), pp. 1–224.

22. "State of the Question," in Hoyt, op. cit., p. 30.

23. *Op. cit.,* p. 37.

24. *Op. cit.,* p. 38.

25. "On the Morality of Birth Control," in Hoyt, *op. cit.,* p. 63.

26. *Op. cit.,* p. 65.

27. *Op. cit.,* p. 67.

28. *Op. cit.,* p. 68.

29. *Op. cit.,* p. 70.

30. *Op. cit.,* p. 71.

31. *Op. cit.,* p. 72.

32. The six theologians were: Alfons Auer, Raymond Sigmund, Paul Anciaux, Michel Labourdette, Joseph Fuchs and Pierre de Locht.

33. Though no official record was kept, it has been reported that the votes of the commission on this document were 52 in favor, 4 opposed.

34. "An Outline for a Document on Responsible Parenthood," in Hoyt, *op. cit.,* p. 86.

35. Hoyt, *op. cit.,* pp. 90–91.

36. "The Papal Commission on Birth Control," *London Tablet,* September 21, 1968.

37. This document was published in the *London Tablet,* September 21, 1968.

38. "The Papal Commission on Birth Control," *op. cit.* Also in Hoyt, *op. cit.,* p. 107.

39. *London Tablet, op. cit.* Also in Hoyt, *op. cit.,* p. 111.

40. Paul VI, "Allocution to the Italian Society of Obstetrics and Gynecology," N.C.W.C. News Service, November 7, 1966.

41. *Ibid.*

42. *Ibid.*

43. *Ibid.*

44. Bruce Stewart, Letter to the Editor, *London Tablet,* November 19, 1966.

45. Paul VI, *Acta Apostolicae Sedis,* July 31, 1964.

VIII THE ENCYCLICAL HUMANAE VITAE

On July 29, 1968, the long-awaited papal statement on birth control was released to the Church and the world. It reaffirmed the traditional position of the Church, repeating the prohibition of contraception that *Casti Connubii* had so firmly asserted thirty-eight years earlier.

Though it reaches the same conclusions as the earlier encyclical and does not go beyond that encyclical in its concept of natural law as the will of God made known through biological rhythms and physiological structure, it nevertheless would be a mistake to describe *Humanae Vitae* as a latter-day *Casti Connubii*. There is a difference of tone and spirit in *Humanae Vitae;* its compassion and pastoral gentleness is in marked contrast to the stern moralism of *Casti Connubii.* There is none of *Casti Connubii's* insistence on the primary and secondary purposes of marriage; instead, the personalist approach to the marriage relationship is fully endorsed and the role of conjugal love in that relationship beautifully portrayed. It freely acknowledges that responsible parenthood is an important and necessary element in married life.

In other words, much of what contemporary theologians have been saying about marriage, Pope Paul is saying too. Apparently, he was keenly aware of the difficult task facing him after he had reached his final dicision to reaffirm the Church's ban on contraception—the task of inserting a prohibition, derived from traditional theology, into the framework of a new, evolving theology of marriage. It seems he was determined, therefore, to put his "No" into a setting of as many "Yeses" as possible. This explains why it is possible for one to read through one-third of the encyclical before beginning to see clearly the direction in which the Pope's thought is moving. There are, in all, thirty-one articles in the encyclical; it is not till the end of Article 10 that one becomes certain that the prohibition on contraception will not be changed.

PART I OF THE ENCYCLICAL: *INTRODUCTION*

Humanae Vitae is divided into three parts The introductory part (Articles 1–6) offers a brief analysis of present-day society and explains the steps that led to the publication of the encyclical.

The encyclical's analysis of the contemporary scene is reminiscent of the initial articles in Vatican II's *Pastoral Constitution on the Church in the Modern World* (*Gaudium et Spes*) and reflects many of the same attitudes. It calls attention to the evolution that has taken place in society and the resultant changes which the Church cannot ignore. Some of the changes enumerated are the population explosion—which many demographers claim poses a threat to the world's future—economic and social changes, changes in the educational needs of children which have placed new burdens on parents, the changing role of women, and the deepened understanding of the importance of conjugal love in marriage.

"This new state of things," the encyclical state, "gives rise to new questions."[1] Three, rooted in the contemporary situation, are proposed:

1. Do these changes indicate that the norms in force up to now need to be revised?

2. Can it be said that the finality of procreation belongs to the totality of conjugal life rather than to its single acts?

3. Has the time come for modern man "to entrust to his reason

and will, rather than the biological rhythms of his organism, the task of regulating birth?"[2]

Whatever reaction one may have to the answers ultimately given to these questions in the encyclical, one cannot accuse Pope Paul of evading the real issues. The most ardent revisionist on the birth control issue could not have stated them more clearly.

These questions, the Pope says, require from the Church "a new and deeper reflection upon the principles of the moral teaching on marriage."[3] It is the duty of the magisterium of the Church, as it is also within its competency, to deal with them, for the Church has received from Christ the responsibility to interpret the entire moral law—not only the law of the Gospel but also the natural law, which are both the expression of God's will for man's moral life. It was the consciousness of this responsibility, he goes on to say, that had prompted him to set up the papal birth control commission and to entrust to it the task of gathering opinions on these important matters. The work of the commission, as well as the advice that he received through consultation with many of the bishops, has furnished the magisterium with a broad base of information that has enabled it to see the many aspects of the problem. All this assistance, however, did not dispense the Pope from the responsibility of a personal examination of the problem. Now, having sifted the documentation given to him, the Pope, "after mature reflection and assiduous prayers," is ready to give his reply to "these grave questions." His reply is given in the remaining two parts of the encyclical, under the titles "Doctrinal Principles" and "Pastoral Directives."

PART II OF THE ENCYCLICAL: *DOCTRINAL PRINCIPLES*

Part II begins with the general principle that any consideration of the birth control problem must go beyond partial perspectives—whether biological, psychological, demographic or sociological—and be placed in the context of a total vision of man and his vocation. Such a total vision of man in the relationship of marriage requires a clear under-standing of the meaning of conjugal love and of responsible parent-hood. In developing these two concepts, the encyclical draws once more on the teaching of *Gaudium et Spes*. The beautiful statement on conjugal love—describing it as human, total, faithful, exclusive, and fecund[4]—offers a personalist view of the husband and wife relationship that clearly acknowledges the growth of this dimension of marriage which found its initial expression in the writings of von Hildebrand and Doms and its official endorsement in Vatican II. Indeed, in a later audience given on August 1, 1968, the Pope explicitly stated that in writing the encyclical, he "willingly adopted the personalist concept which is proper to the Council's doctrine on conjugal society and which gives to the love that generates and nourishes it the preeminent place that befits it in the subjective evaluation of marriage."[5]

Responsible parenthood is presented in Article 10 as the necessary context in which conjugal love can find its true fulfillment. The exercise of responsible parenthood requires that husband and wife "recognize their duties toward God, toward themselves, toward the family, and toward society, in a correct hierarchy of values."[6]

Up to this point, i.e., the second last paragraph of Article 10, the encyclical could have moved in either direction—toward a change in the Church's teaching on contraception or toward a reaffirmation of the norms of the past. There are intimations in Articles 6 and 7 of the Pope's ultimate stand but, as previously mentioned, it begins to emerge only in the last paragraph of Article 10 where it is stated that husband and wife, in the exercise of responsible parenthood, are not free to determine "in a wholly autonomous way the honest path to follow. . . . They must conform their activity to the creative intention of God expressed in the very nature of marriage and its acts and manifested by the constant teaching of the Church."[7]

In Article 11, the Pope unmistakably takes his stand with the tradition of the past when he says: "The Church, calling men back to the observance of the norms of the natural law, as interpreted by her constant doctrine, teaches that each and every marriage act must remain open to the transmission of life."[8]

This is not to suggest that there is necessarily a contradiction between Article 11 and what precedes it. It simply means that although the Pope asserts that due respect must be given to the interpersonal dimension of marriage, he nonetheless insists that sexuality in marriage can never be considered as an exclusively interpersonal value. This interpersonal dimension of married love, deserving of respect in itself, must in turn respect the creative design of God "inscribed in the very being of man and woman."[9]

This creative design of God, "expressed in the very nature of marriage and its acts,"[10] forbids the deliberate separation of the husband and wife love union from the fruitfulness to which that union is ordered. There is, in other words, "an inseparable connection, willed by God and unable to be broken by man on his own initiative, between the two meanings of the conjugal act: the unitive meaning and the procreative meaning."[11]

The operative word here, of course, is "inseparable." The advocates of change in the Church's teaching on contraception do not deny that there is a connection between conjugal love and procreation; what they do deny is that the connection is inseparable. They affirm that while both the unitive and procreative meaning of marriage must be respected, there are times when, for the good of marriage in its totality, the value of procreation must be sacrificed to the value of conjugal love.

It is precisely this view which the encyclical rejects on the grounds that deliberate interference with the natural processes which precede, accompany or follow the act of intercourse is to violate the design of the Creator.[12] It is to treat as belonging exclusively to the married couple a faculty which was intended to associate them in a unique way with the Author of life. In words that recall the fundamental position set forth in the working paper drawn up by the papal commission's minority group, the encyclical declares: "Just as man does not have unlimited dominion over his body in general, so also, with particular reason, he has not such dominion over his generative faculties as such, because of their intrinsic ordination toward raising up life, of which God is the principle."[13]

Whatever the encyclical may have said about conjugal love (Article 9), Articles 11 to 15 make clear that that love must always be subordinated to the "natural laws and rhythms of fecundity."[14] The physiological structure of intercourse is an expression of the will of God; it can never be violated by the deliberate will of man.

Three Positions Rejected

The encyclical mentions (Articles 14–16) three positions defended by those who advocate a modification of the Church's teaching. These positions are:

1. There are times when married couples must choose contraception as the lesser of two evils.

2. Individual conjugal acts that are rendered materially infertile by human intervention derive a formal fertility from their orientation to the fertility of marriage as a whole.

3. Man is called by God, not simply to submit to natural processes, but to use his reason to control nature for a human good.

The encyclical rejects these positions but makes no detailed effort to refute them. It also rejects abortion and sterilization as legitimate means of birth control. At the same time it repeats the traditional approval of rhythm as a licit means of family planning when serious reasons justify its use, and reaffirms the traditional distinction between contraception and rhythm that the former involves a deliberate interference with man's natural processes, while the latter does not. Contraception, therefore, can never be justified.

The Consequences of Contraception

In Article 17 Pope Paul speaks of the serious consequences that would follow the use of artificial birth control. He first says that it would lead to moral laxity. "A wide and easy road would thus be opened toward conjugal infidelity and the general lowering of morality."[15] It would, moreover, disrupt the interpersonal relationship of husband and wife because a mna, growing accustomed to contraceptive practices would tend to hold his wife in less esteem, even to the point of "considering her as a mere instrument of selfish enjoyment, and no longer as his respected and beloved companion."[16] The encyclical thus turns against the advocates of contraception one of the arguments that they had used to defend it—that the interpersonal relationship of marriage is often seriously threatened when the option of contraception is not open to a couple.

The encyclical sees yet another danger that would accompany the acceptance of contraception: marriage would be threatened not only from within, but also from without, for contraception would place "a dangerous weapon" in the hands of "those public authorities who take no heed of moral exigencies."[17] Placed at the mercy of intervention by public authorities would be "the most personal and the most reserved sector of conjugal intimacy," because, the encyclical asks, "Who will stop rulers from favoring, from even imposing, upon their peoples, if they were to consider it necessary, the method of contraception which they judge to be most efficacious?"[18]

The doctrinal section of the encyclical concludes with what many will consider a note of moral righteousness not unlike the famous passage in *Casti Connubii* which describes the Church as that "to whom God has entrusted the defense of the integrity and purity of morals, standing in the midst of the moral ruin which surrounds her."[19] *Humanae Vitae* concedes that its teaching will not be readily received by all, because:

. . . too numerous are those voices—amplified by the modern means to propaganda—which are contrary to the voice of the Church. . . . To tell the truth, the Church is not surprised to be made, like her divine Founder, a "sign of contradiction," yet she does not because of this cease to proclaim with humble firmness the entire moral law, both natural and evangelical. Of such laws the Church was not the author, nor consequently can she be their arbiter; she is only their depositary and their interpreter, without ever being able to declare to be licit that which is not so by reason of its intimate and unchangeable opposition to the true good of man. In defending conjugal morals in their integral wholeness, the Church knows that she contributes toward the establishment of truly human civilization.[20]

PART III OF THE ENCYCLICAL: *PASTORAL DIRECTIVES*

Part III of the encyclical (Articles 19–31) is a strong appeal to various groups in the Church and in the world to receive the encyclical and to implement its teachings. Educators are called upon to create an atmosphere that fosters rather than threatens chastity. Public authorities are urged not to permit the introduction by legislation of "practices contrary to the natural and divine law . . . into that fundamental cell, the family."[21] Men of science as well as physicians and medical personnel are invited to use their skills and pool their efforts in order to provide "a sufficiently secure basis for a regulation of births, founded on the observance of natural rhythms."[22] Christian husbands and wives are urged to be docile to the voice of the Church, remembering that "their Christian vocation, which began at baptism, is further specified and reinforced by the sacrament of matrimony," and "if sin should still keep its hold on them," they should not be discouraged, but "have recourse with humble perseverance to the mercy of God, which is poured forth in the sacrament of penance."[23]

A special admonition is directed to priests as "the counselors and spiritual guides of individual persons and families."[24] They are exhorted to rally to the support of the magisterium and to expound its teachings in unity and without ambiguity. In thus speaking with one voice, they will give the faithful an example of loyal obedience to the Church's teaching and thereby contribute to peace of consciences and unity among God's people. They must guard against diluting the saving teaching of Christ; yet, at the same time, in presenting that teaching they must share in the patience and gentleness of Him who came, not to judge the world, but to save it. This will mean that married couples, whatever difficulties they encounter, will always find "in the words and in the heart of a priest, the echo of the voice and the love of the Redeemer."[25]

Finally, Pope Paul addresses himself to his fellow bishops. He urges them "to work ardently and incessantly for the safeguarding of the holiness of marriage, so that it may always be lived in its entire human and Christian fullness."[26] This, he reminds them, is one of their most urgent responsibilities, calling for concerted pastoral action in all fields of human activity—economic, cultural, and social—since it is only by improving man's lot in these various areas that it will be possible "to render the life of parents and of children within their families, not only tolerable, but easier and more joyous."[27]

THE AUTHORITY OF THE ENCYCLICAL

The intention of the encyclical was to settle a question that had long been debated within the Church; however, its immediate result was to open up a whole new series of questions within the Catholic community: What was the authority of the encyclical? Does the theological position favoring contraception still have probability? What were now the rights of individual conscience? Would a Catholic be justified in following his conscience if it conflicted with the norms laid down by the encyclical?

These questions became the subject of lively debate in the Church. Before discussing the details of that debate among bishops, theologians and lay people, it may be useful to consider the remarks of two theologians whose close association with the Vatican give special weight to their words.

Msgr. Ferdinando Lambruschini

Msgr. Ferdinando Lambruschini, professor of moral theology at the Lateran University, was the Vatican spokesman who, at a press conference on July 29, 1968, made public the text of *Humanae Vitae*. The choice of Msgr. Lambruschini to present the encyclical was particularly significant, since he had been a member of the papal birth control commission and was known to have sided with those theologians who advocated a change in the Church's teaching. The fact that he was chosen to present a document whose content he had initially opposed was evidence of a strong desire on the part of the Holy See to close ranks within the Church on the issue of birth control.

In his formal remarks to the press, Msgr. Lambruschini made it clear that the encyclical is not an infallible document; he made it equally clear, however, that this did not mean that the problem of birth regulation remains "in a condition of vague problematics."[28] Even though not infallible, the encyclical is an authentic pronouncement of the magisterium and, as such, it requires "loyal and full assent, both interior and exterior"[29] on the part of Catholics. He continued:

Those who in recent times incautiously believed, even in good faith, that they could teach the lawfulness of using artificial contraceptive practices for the regulation of births and behaved accordingly in pastoral directives and in the ministry of confession, must change their views and give the example by full adhesion to the teachings of the encyclical. It is not a question of deplorable servility but of a necessary loyalty and consistency in the profession of Catholic teaching and in the practice of the Christian life.[30]

While insisting on the authoritative character of the encyclical, Msgr. Lambruschini, in a press interview following his formal remarks, added that the encyclical did not necessarily close the issue for all time. The Associated Press quoted him as saying: "The rule [against artificial birth control] is not unreformable. It is up to theologians to debate and expand all moral aspects involved; and if, for instance, some principle should become overwhelmingly accepted in the Church, contraception may even be launched."[31]

Ladislaus Orsy, S.J., professor of canon law at Fordham University,

New York, suggested that Msgr. Lambruschini could hardly have made his statement "without probably the highest previous approval." He added that "the Church authorities were apparently very careful not to commit themselves too much for the future."[32]

Gustave Martelet, S.J.

At a Paris press conference on the day of the encyclical's release, and later in a letter to the editor of the *London Sunday Times,* Father Gustave Martelet, a French theologian, offered some significant remarks on the relationship between the encyclical and individual conscience. His remarks are of special importance, since he was reported to have assisted in the preparation of *Humanae Vitae.* Martelet pointed out that "An encyclical does not contain the answers to every question. It is not a book of recipes." As was the case before the publication of the encyclical, he said, "many difficulties remain and it is for every man and woman to resolve them in the secrecy of his or her heart."[33]

In his letter to the *Sunday Times,* Father Martelet underscored the fact that the teaching of the encyclical cannot be simply a substitute for individual conscience. The Pope's intention in writing the encyclical, he said, was "not to restrict conscience, but to clarify it." His letter continued:

No one, evidently, can usurp the decision that married couples will make. In this sense they are, after as before the encyclical, the creatures of their own conscience. Who is not? But their consciences can now know what is certain on a difficult and long debated point, its *inalienable norm,* even if, for one reason or another, that conscience finds it impossible to subscribe to that norm.[34]

NOTES

1. Paul VI, *Humanae Vitae,* Art. 3. (All selections from *Humanae Vitae* used in this book are from the translation of the *United States Catholic Conference* (Washington, D.C.).)

2. *Ibid.*

3. *Op. cit.,* Art. 4.

4. *Op. cit.,* Art. 9.

5. "The Church in the World," *London Tablet,* August 10, 1968.

6. *Op. cit.,* Art. 10.

7. *Ibid.*

8. *Op. cit.,* Art. 11.

9. *Op. cit.,* Art. 12.

10. *Op. cit.,* Art. 10.

11. *Op. cit.,* Art. 12.

12. *Op. cit.,* Art. 14.

13. *Op. cit.,* Art. 13.

14. *Op. cit.,* Art. 11.

15. *Op. cit.,* Art. 17.

16. *Ibid.*

17. *Ibid.*

18. *Ibid.*

19. Pius XI, *Casti Connubii,* Art. 57.

20. Paul VI, *op. cit.,* Art. 18.

21. *Op. cit.,* Art. 23.

22. *Op. cit.,* Art. 24.

23. *Op. cit.,* Art. 25. The pastoral solicitude of *Humanae Vitae* is in sharp contrast to the severity of the moral judgment passed in *Casti Connubii* on the faithful who practice birth control and on the priests who fail to deter them from such practices.

24. *Op. cit.,* Art. 28.

25. *Op. cit.,* Art. 29.

26. *Op. cit.,* Art. 30.

27. *Ibid.*

28. N. C. News Service, August 8, 1968.

29. *Ibid.*

30. *Ibid.*

31. *The* (Davenport) *Catholic Messenger,* August 1, 1968.

32. *Op. cit.,* August 8, 1968.

33. *London Sunday Times,* August 4, 1968.

34. Gustave Martelet, Letter to the Editor, *London Sunday Times,* August 18, 1968.

IX THE BISHOPS AND THE ENCYCLICAL

The Second Vatican Council was clear in its teaching of the principle of collegiality: the bishops constitute a stable body, or "college," and this college of bishops, with the Pope as its head, is collectively responsible for the tasks of the whole Church. The Council did not, however, give any clear answer to the question of how this principle would operate. One may speculate that the reason for the omission was that the fathers themselves were not certain of what the answer should be. They might have felt that only the living experience of the Church could spell out what it meant for the Church to function in a collegial way.

Collegiality does not seem to have been involved to any notable degree in the writing of the encyclical *Humanae Vitae*. It is true that the Pope speaks in the encyclical of "the successive judgments and counsels spontaneously forwarded by or expressly requested from a good number of our brothers in the episcopate."[1] Yet his action in withdrawing the topic of birth regulation from the agenda of the Council and reserving the decision to himself would seem to indicate that it was not his intention to deal with this question collegially.

It seems correct to say, however, that in the many and varied reactions of the bishops to the papal pronouncement on birth control, we are able to see the principle of collegiality operating in the Church *post factum,* since the episcopal statements on the encyclical have introduced a new phenomenon into the life of the Church; national conferences of bishops not merely echoing the contents of a papal document, but interpreting that content and, in some cases, departing from certain of its elements. This gives promise that collegiality is on the way toward becoming a part of the experience of the Church.

This chapter will attempt to do two things: first, to summarize the statements of various national bodies of bishops, and, secondly, to comment on the significance of these statements.

THE DUTCH BISHOPS

The first reaction of a national body of bishops came from the Netherlands. On August 2, 1968, Cardinal Bernard Alfrink and the six other bishops issued a joint letter addressed to the Dutch clergy, offering guidelines to assist them in presenting the encyclical to the people.

The letter notes the unrest among many Roman Catholics and the general disappointment with the stand taken in *Humanae Vitae* on the question of contraceptives; at the same time the bishops point out the positive values of marriage—among them the defense of the dignity of life and the appeal for responsibility in marriage—which the encyclical affirms.

Because the encyclical is an authoritative, though not infallible document, individual conscience cannot ignore it. On the other hand, the bishops declare, there are "already many factors which determine one's personal conscience regarding marriage rules, for example, mutual love, relations in the family, and social circumstances."[2]

The bishops express the hope that the discussion on the papal letter will "contribute to a better functioning of authority within the Church."[3]

THE MEXICAN BISHOPS

On August 9 the hierarchy of Mexico, following their annual meeting, pledged their support to the Pope and to his encyclical. They point out that the encyclical is "not simply an opinion from which it is permissible to dissent," but "a solemn confirmation of a constant teaching of the Church."[4]

They reject the criticism that the encyclical shows little understanding of the problems involved in married life and caution Catholics that "it is never licit to accept the opinions of theologians against a constant teaching of the Church."[5]

THE GERMAN BISHOPS

The German bishops, after a two-day meeting held in Koenigstein on August 29-30, issued a pastoral statement on the encyclical. This statement draws attention to the positive teaching set forth in the encyclical: its concern for the whole man, its stress on the dignity of man and the sanctity of human life, its affirmation of conjugal love and responsible parenthood. At the same time the bishops acknowledge that no encyclical of recent decades has aroused so much opposition as *Humanae Vitae*. They find this opposition understandable in view of the fact that during the long period of time that the encyclical was in preparation, a new theological and pastoral atmosphere had been created, leading many people to expect a different decision from the Holy Father.

Turning to the question of the encyclical's authority, the bishops declare that because encyclicals are utterances of the teaching Church, every Catholic is obligated to accept the teaching of *Humanae Vitae*, "even if he has formed a prior different opinion."[6] The fact that many Christians all over the world—bishops, priests, and married couples—have complied with the encyclical's demands and have made its teaching their own is a significant sign that should not be overlooked. On the other hand, the bishops continue, "many are of the opinion that they cannot accept the encyclical's statement on the methods of regulating birth."[7] They grant that a man may in good conscience deviate from a non-infallible teaching, but they warn that the person who would do so "must question his conscience soberly and critically as to whether he can justify this before God."[8] Though offering this warning, they nevertheless admonish pastors "to respect in their work, especially in the administration of the sacraments, the decision of conscience of the believers made in the awareness of their responsibility."[9]

The bishops stress the need for further dialogue in the Church, pointing out that criticism, while sometimes negative and destructive, can also be a "beneficial, purifying process." They promise that they will do their best to further dialogue and in a spirit of collegiality "will carry on conversations with the Holy Father and with the episcopates of other countries."[10]

THE BELGIAN BISHOPS

The Belgian hierarchy issued a two-part statement on the encyclical, with a postscript, at Malines on August 30. The first part discusses the meaning of the encyclical. Noting "the lively interest" and "the difference of opinion" which the encyclical has evoked, the bishops strongly recommend a thorough reading of the document and careful reflection on its contents. Such study will reveal that the encyclical is a comprehensive document that presents "an integral view of man in regard to marriage and the family," and emphasizes "two aspects which are positive and essential: conjugal love and responsible parenthood."[11] These positive values of marriage constitute the core of the encyclical's teaching; therefore, it would be most unfortunate if these considerations were neglected and attention given to only that part of the document which prohibits contraception.

On the other hand, this prohibition of artificial methods of birth control, coming as it does from the supreme authority of the Church, cannot be ignored. It constitutes "a rule of conduct for the Catholic conscience and no one is authorized to dispute that its character is in itself obligatory."[12]

The authoritative nature of the encyclical, however, does not dispense the bishops from their pastoral responsibility toward those of he faithful who are "deeply distressed by certain demands of the encyclical" and who are asking "to what extent they are bound to accept and observe the directives given by the Pope."[13] Addressing themselves to this pastoral problem in the second part of their statement, the bishops recall the principles laid down in *Lumen Gentium*,[14] which govern the interpretation of documents that emanate from the teaching authority of the Church. Three principles are given, which may be summarized as follows:

1. Every doctrinal declaration of the teaching Church must be received with respect and in a spirit of docility and openness.

2. Infallible statements must be adhered to with the obedience of faith.

3. Statements that are authoritative, but not infallible, require a religious submission of mind and will; they cannot, however, demand "an unconditional and absolute adherence."[15]

Applying these principles to the encyclical, the bishops advise that one "who is competent in the matter under consideration and capable of forming a personal and well-founded judgment . . . may, after a serious examination before God, come to other conclusions on certain points."[16] In such a case, a person has the right to follow his conviction, provided he remains sincerely disposed to further inquiry; but he should maintain his adherence to Christ and the Church, and acknowledge the importance of the Church's supreme teaching authority.

The bishops' statement also considers the problem of a conflict of duties—a situation that may exist when the faithful sincerely believe that they cannot conform to the directives of the encyclical. If they fail at first to adapt their conduct to these directives, they should not on that account consider themselves separated from God's love.

In the postscript to their statement, the bishops admit that there are arguments proposed in the encyclical—some relating to principles, others concerning the consequences of contraceptive practices—which not everyone will accept as valid, and it should not be assumed that those who find these arguments unconvincing "are acting out of selfish or hedonistic motives."[17] The postscript also recalls the traditional teaching that the ultimate practical norm of action is a duly enlightened conscience.

THE BISHOPS OF CEYLON

In a joint 750-word pastoral letter issued in September, Cardinal Thomas Cooray and nine other bishops of Ceylon called for the "full and loyal assent"[18] of the country's Catholics to Pope Paul's encyclical. "Our conscience as Catholics," the letter reads, "does not allow us to accept as moral all means of birth control."[19] These means include various measures for family planning initiated by the government, although the very existence of government family planning agencies is indicative of how widespread is the concern over a truly human problem which involves the good of the individual, the family and the nation itself.

The bishops strongly disapprove of criticisms of the encyclical based on arguments completely outside the moral sphere. The Holy Father, they say, "was fully aware of these partial perspectives whether of the biological or psychological, demographic or sociological orders."[20]

The pastoral concludes with a warning to Catholics against disobeying the Pope's directives; it reminds them that it was the disobedience of the first Adam that brought destruction to the world, as it was the obedience of he second Adam that brought salvation.

THE ITALIAN BISHOPS

The Conference of Italian bishops released a two-thousand-word statement on September 10 in which they expressed their full communion of faith and purpose with the Vicar of Christ and their profound gratitude for his well-weighed and enlightened pronouncement.

Though fully appreciative of the fact that study, contemplation and the experience of the faithful deepen the Church's understanding of

God's will, the bishops nevertheless counsel that this understanding finds true expression and guidance in the teaching of the Roman Pontiff and the bishops in communion with him. For this reason the encyclical, which represents the authentic teaching of the Sovereign Pontiff on a matter reserved to his decision by the Council, must be received with religious submission of minds and wills.

Though the encyclical is not a complete treatment of marriage and the family, it does apply to the problem of birth control the general teaching of the Church that marriage is a community of spouses ordered to generous and responsible fruitfulness. Since it is part of that teaching that men are not "unconditionally masters of their body and its functions," the encyclical's clear instruction is that "the natural order willed by God"[21] must always be respected in the conjugal act. Although this is not the sole criterion for spouses to live by, it must be safeguarded as an indispensable element of Christian perfection in marriage.

The encyclical, by protecting and promoting the partnership of married life and love, expresses the Church's maternal care for the general and personal good of mankind; at the same time it is open to further perspectives which may favor honest regulation of human procreation.

The bishops address themselves to three groups in the Church—theologians, priests and married couples. The theologians, who are entitled to "proper freedom of research," are asked to give loyal adherence to the encyclical's teaching and to cooperate with the magisterium in helping the faithful understand that teaching. They are also urged to develop those points of moral teaching not touched upon in the encyclical.

Priests in the pastoral ministry are called upon to apply the teaching of the encyclical without ambiguity or discord. At the same time they are to treat penitents with compassion and understanding, especially those who fail to comply with the directives of the encyclical because of honest difficulties experienced in their efforts to reconcile responsible parenthood and mutual love. The failure of such persons to conform to the Christian norm, "cannot surely be equated in its serious importance with that which might spring solely from motives vitiated by egotism and hedonism."[22]

Compassion and understanding on the part of confessors, however, must be held within reasonable bounds in order to avoid the possibility of fostering in spouses "mediocre behavior or facile compromises." All Christians are called to a persevering and responsible effort to fulfill God's will.

Finally, the bishops exhort Christian spouses to accept the teachings of the Vicar of Christ in a spirit of faith and as an essential element in the formation of their consciences. Difficulties encountered in putting these teachings into practice must be seen by the faithful as God's invitation to participate in the Cross of the Lord Jesus. They should also remember that there are laws of growth in the attainment of virtue and at times, in striving for the ideal, one will pass through stages of imperfection.

THE EAST GERMAN BISHOPS

The East German bishops, in their statement on the encyclical, urge obedience to the Pope. Though the Pope does not speak in the encyclical with the highest authority of his teaching office, "we cannot," the bishops declare, "use the non-infallibility of the encyclical as a starting point for discussion."[23] Nor can such discussions start from the assumption that a person is free to deviate from the papal rule.

Priests are instructed to uphold the papal directive, but to avoid any display of arrogance toward those "who believe they can hold another judgment of conscience."[24]

THE AUSTRIAN BISHOPS

Following a two-day meeting at Graz (September 20–21), the Austrian bishops presented their views on *Humanae Vitae*. Taking note of the worldwide reverberations of both approval and criticism that has followed the publication of the encyclical, the bishops speak of the uneasiness that has gripped many Catholics and of the questions they have voiced to which, "it is not easy to provide answers at the present time."[25]

The Holy Father in *Humanae Vitae* has drawn a lofty image of marriage—on the one hand rejecting all self-seeking and abuse of human sexuality and, on the other, stressing the twofold meaning of marriage: the personal giving of self and the engendering of new life. These two meanings form an inner unity which brings maturity to the spouses in their personalities and associates them with God in the continuation of the human race.

This inner unity of marriage obligates husband and wife to responsible parenthood, which means that they themselves "can determine, in their consciences formed before God,"[26] the number of children they will have. Forming their consciences before God requires that "the reasons for the limitation of children must be of a moral nature."[27] It would be wrong, therefore, to avoid children for the sake of convenience or selfishness. "Conscience may not be replaced by chemical means."[28]

What is the binding character of the encyclical and its role in the formation of conscience? In answering this question, the bishops affirm the teaching of Vatican II that requires religious submission of mind and will to authentic pronouncements of the magisterium. The bishops at the same time affirm freedom of conscience, but emphasize that this is not the same thing as freedom in the formation of conscience. In the formation of conscience man is bound by the law of God, and one of the functions of the magisterium is to enlighten man's understanding of that law. One may not, therefore, in the formation of his conscience, overlook the teaching of the Church.

Since the encyclical is not infallible, however, it is conceivable that some may feel unable to accept its teaching. In such a case a person with experience in dogma who has reached a mature conviction divergent from the teaching of the encyclical, may follow his conscience as long as he remains open to further study and does not create confusion for others.

The bishops also point out that in the encyclical the Holy Father does not speak of grave sin. Hence "if someone should err against the teaching of the encyclical, he must not feel cut off from God's love in every case, and may receive Holy Communion without first going to confession."[29]

THE BISHOPS OF ENGLAND AND WALES

A statement on *Humanae Vitae* by the bishops of England and Wales was released on September 24 following a two-day meeting. Mindful of the "strong feeling" that has been aroused by the encyclical, the bishops counsel responsible and temperate discussion in a spirit of charity.

They regret that so much of the discussion thus far has centered mainly on the question of contraception to the neglect of the positive teachings on marriage that are so evident in the encyclical. The faithful and their pastors are urged to study the document as a whole.

Several paragraphs are devoted to a defense of Pope Paul and his right to decide personally the issue of birth regulation. "In the heat of controversy," the bishops state, "some writers have forgotten that the Pope is the Vicar of Christ. It is for him to issue encyclical letters whenever he thinks it his duty to do so."[30] Some have forgotten, too, that the encyclical was the fruit, not only of prayer, but of years of consultation with bishops, theologians, doctors, scientists and married couples. Though admitting that collegiality was not involved in the writing of the encyclical, the bishops declare that this cannot be invoked as a reason for refusing to give assent to the encyclical, for it had been generally recognized at the Council that "a question of such delicacy as contraception could not properly be debated in that vast assembly."[31]

The bishops recognize that because of the theological controversies of recent years many people, anticipating a different statement from the Pope, have come to rely on contraceptives and now are unable to see that their use, at least in their own personal circumstances, is wrong. Such persons should bear in mind "the great weight which attaches to a pronouncement from the Holy Father,"[32] and, instead of closing their minds, should keep them open to the influence of the Holy Spirit. They should realize, too, that the Holy Father was well aware of the difficulties faced by married people; this is why the encyclical recalls the compassion and gentleness of the Lord and contains no sweeping condemnations or threats of damnation. Far from being excluded from the sacraments, those who experience difficulties are invited to receive them more frequently.

The bishops' statement stops short of saying explicitly that Catholics may in conscience dissent from the encyclical, but they make it clear that in any discussion of the binding force of the encyclical "the primacy of conscience is not in dispute. The Pope, bishops, clergy and faithful must all be true to conscience. . . . Neither this encyclical nor any other document of the Church takes away from us our right and duty to follow our conscience."[33] What is involved in the present issue is the obligation to do everything in our power to make sure that our conscience is truly informed. "If we were to neglect the guidance of the Church, morality could easily become merely subjective. This would be disastrous."[34]

THE SPANISH BISHOPS

A statement, on September 27, of the Spanish Bishops' Committee on Doctrine and Faith expressed "deep regret that even in Spain opinions are being espoused that are in sharp disagreement with the basic teachings of Pope Paul's encyclical, *Humanae Vitae*."[35] The committee declared that "any doctrine, even if it comes from noted theologians or ecclesiastical personalities, which runs counter to the teaching authority of the Pope, is devoid of authority and cannot be taken as a norm for personal conscience."[36]

Later, in November, after a nine-day meeting in Madrid, the bishops issued a joint statement calling on Catholics to accept the teachings of the encyclical "not as a dogmatic definition, but as a clear and simple question of faith and morals."[37] They acknowledge that there may be circumstances in which the responsibility of persons practicing birth control may be diminished, but insist that contraceptive acts are contrary to the divine and natural law and are, therefore, in themselves objectively immoral.

THE CANADIAN BISHOPS

In their statement on the encyclical, published in the *Canadian Register* on October 5, the Canadian bishops express their unity with the Pope in his teaching on the dignity of married life. They share also the pastoral concern which led him to offer counsel and guidance to the faithful in a most important area of human life. They declare also their unity with the people of God in the difficulties they have experienced in understanding the encyclical, in making its teaching their own, and in living by that teaching.

The bishops admit that many Catholics face a serious crisis of conscience in their efforts to accept the teaching of the encyclical because in recent years grave doubts have arisen concerning the validity of the arguments advanced to forbid any positive intervention in the transmission of life.

Pointing to Vatican II's description of conscience as "the most secret core and sanctuary of a man," where he is "alone with God whose voice echoes in his depths,"[38] they assert that "the dignity of man consists precisely in his ability to achieve his fulfillment in God through the exercise of a knowing and free choice."[39] On the other hand, the bishops caution that freedom of conscience does not exempt a man from the obligation of forming his conscience according to truly Christian values and principles, free from selfishness and from undue external pressures which are incompatible with the spirit of Christ.

The formation of a true Christian conscience demands a cheerful readiness to listen to the Church. Since the Holy Father has spoken on the question of morally acceptable means of harmonizing conjugal love and responsible parenthood, "Christians must examine in all honesty their reactions to what he said,"[40] keeping in mind their responsibility to give religious submission of mind and will to the authentic teaching of the Roman Pontiff.

It must also be recognized, the bishops state, that a number of Catholics find it extremely difficult, or even impossible, to accept everything taught in the encyclical. This difficulty must be given sympathetic understanding. Since these people are not denying any point of divine and Catholic faith or rejecting the teaching authority of the Church, they should not be considered by others or themselves as cut off from the body of the faithful. They must, however, sincerely examine their motives and continue to study the Church's teachings.

In discussing pastoral practice, the bishops appeal to confessors and counsellors to show "sympathetic understanding and reverence for the sincere good faith of those who fail in their efforts to accept some point of the encyclical."[41] Moreover, the bishops continue, it accords with accepted principles of moral theology to say that those who experience what seems to them to be a clear conflict of duties may be assured that "whoever honestly chooses that course which seems right to him does so in good conscience."[42]

The bishops conclude their statement with an appeal for unity, which does not lie "in a bland conformity in all ideas," but rather "in a union of faith and heart, in submission to God's will, and a humble but honest and ongoing search for the truth."[43] Such an understanding of unity demands a love that is willing to place all one's intelligence at the service of the Church. "If this sometimes means that in our desire to make the Church more intelligible and more beautiful, we must, as pilgrims do, falter in the way or differ as to the way, no one should conclude that our common faith is lost or our loving purpose blunted."[44]

THE BISHOPS OF SCOTLAND

On October 7, following their semi-annual meeting at St. Mary's College, Blairs, the bishops of Scotland issued a joint pastoral letter on *Humanae Vitae*. In it they indicate their intention of giving, not a commentary on the encyclical, but some guiding principles that should be kept in mind while reading it. They feel it their duty to offer such guidelines, because criticism and opposition to the encyclical has created surprise and confusion among the faithful.

They begin with a reminder that the Church has divine authority to teach and guide the faithful in matters of faith and morals, and one of the ways in which this authority is exercised is through the teaching of the pope. Not all papal statements, however, carry equal weight or authority; each document has to be judged in the light of the matter with which it deals and by the manner in which the pope speaks. In *Humanae Vitae* the matter is of the utmost gravity and Pope Paul has spoken in virtue of his office as supreme pastor and teacher. His teaching, therefore, demands acceptance by the faithful. They must give to it the allegiance of mind and will that is due to the authentic magisterium of the Roman Pontiff.

The bishops assert that man has the right and duty to follow his conscience. But, they add, this right must be properly understood. "Man is not a law to himself; his conscience is not completely independent."[45] The role of conscience is to judge the morality of our actions on the basis of sound principles of right and wrong. The encyclical provides such principles and it is according to these that Catholics are to form their consciences. This obligation is not an offense against freedom of conscience; rather it is implicit in the free decision to accept the claim of the Catholic Church that She speaks with the authority of Christ.

The bishops are not unmindful of the pressing problems that arise in married life or of the weaknesses inherent in human nature. They are aware of the desire of their people to be faithful to Christ, and like Christ, they want to encourage rather than condemn. In this spirit they offer their assurance to those who accept the Church's teaching, but who fail at times through human weakness to live according to that teaching, that they need not fear meeting Christ in the sacrament of forgiveness.

They exhort Catholics, especially married couples, to read and study the encyclical in its entirety. It involves much more than a prohibition; it is a moving appeal from the Holy Father for a deeper understanding of the holiness of Christian marriage and of the true meaning of Christian love. "His advice and counsel," they say, "will go far to comfort and strengthen those who experience great difficulties and problems in their married life."[46]

THE BISHOPS OF IRELAND

A two-day meeting at Maynooth by the bishops of Ireland brought forth on October 9 a statement calling upon Catholics to accept the encyclical and to give it that "wholehearted assent which the Second Vatican Council requires."[47] They remind their people that the Pope speaks not as one theologian among many, but as the Vicar of Christ who has the special assistance of the Holy Spirit and who is simply reaffirming in the encyclical what the Church has always taught on contraception.

The bishops take no stand of their own regarding the role of conscience. They merely cite two passages from *Gaudium et Spes*—the one requiring that consciences be conformed to the divine law and submissive to the teaching authority of the Church, and the other forbidding spouses to employ methods of birth regulation found blameworthy by the Church.[48]

They acknowledge that the encyclical may have created personal problems and intellectual difficulties for some; but they call for an appreciation of its teaching as a whole and further assure their people that priests, especially in the confessional, "will, without compromise of principle, show that understanding and sympathy which our divine Lord Himself always displayed."[49]

THE BISHOPS OF INDIA

At the conclusion of a five-day meeting at Bangalore, India, the bishops pledged their support of the encyclical.[50] They called upon priests and laity to publicize its contents in unequivocal terms and to hold steadfast to its principles. The Church, they go on to say, will cooperate with the government in advancing the idea of responsible parenthood as a means of controlling population growth; at the same time they entreat the government not to victimize those who conscientiously object to the means adopted by the government in its family-planning campaign.

THE SCANDINAVIAN BISHOPS

The bishops of Denmark, Finland, Norway, and Sweden met in Stockholm, and on October 17 announced their reactions to *Humanae Vitae*. In their statement they express their awareness of the criticism engendered by the encyclical and their realization that it comes not only from those who consider pleasure the highest aim of life, but also from men of good will who are conscious of their responsibility to marriage and society.

After accentuating the positive message of the encyclical, the bishops turn their attention to two questions that are in the minds of many Catholics: With what authority does the encyclical speak? May a Catholic hold another opinion?

The bishops in their reply make the familiar distinction between statements of the Church that bear the mark of infallibility and those that do not. Since there have been occasions in the history of the Church when statements in non-infallible documents have been later rectified or amplified, such a possibility cannot, in principle, be excluded in the case of *Humanae Vitae,* which is recognized by everyone as containing no infallible definition. Nevertheless, according to the teaching of Vatican II, even those papal documents that do not claim infallibility require religious submission of mind and will. This means that the faithful must be positively receptive to what is taught. No one, therefore, should question the contents of the encyclical without first having studied it adequately and prayerfully. However, the statement continues: "Should someone . . . for grave and carefully considered reasons, not feel able to subscribe to the arguments of the encyclical, he is entitled, as has been constantly acknowledged, to entertain other views than those put forward in a non-infallible declaration of the Church."[51]

Such a person, ultimately, is answerable to God for his attitudes and conduct, and should not, because of the decision he feels obliged to make, be regarded on that account as an inferior Catholic.

In speaking of the rights of conscience, the bishops first point out that one's conscience must be properly formed and matured. Then they add: "Man should never under any circumstances act against his conscience. . . . No one, not even the Church, is entitled to dispense him from the duty of obeying his conscience and carrying the responsibility for so doing."[52]

In a time of rapid evolution toward an unknown future, the bishops plead for unity in essentials and for fidelity to the Gospel of Christ. They urge the faithful to preserve a sense of proportion, "for the world of today presents greater problems than the question of how precisely these intimate aspects of marriage should be regulated."[53] Whatever differences Christians may have on this subject, there are far more important areas of agreement in the overall understanding of marriage and the dignity of the human person.

So long as this sense of proportion is preserved, a certain divergence of opinion may even be necessary and beneficial. . . . All exchange of opinion demands tolerance in the true sense of this word. Let us accept that others have a right to their opinions, and let us help them carry their burden.[54]

THE BISHOPS OF THE PHILIPPINE ISLANDS

In a lengthy and somewhat rambling statement the Filipino bishops, on October 22, expressed their wholehearted endorsement of the encyclical. The Holy Father, they state, has given "the right moral guidance."[55] His children in Christ must accept his word with filial love and follow it faithfully and loyally. The encyclical is "the best defense of itself,"[56] and a Catholic who reads it with an open mind, free from the prejudices propagated by the defenders of artificial birth control, cannot fail to be convinced by the soundness of the Pope's position.

Refusal to accept the encyclical is a serious matter of disobedience, and no one can justify disobedience to the Pope's teaching on the grounds that he must follow his conscience. Conscience is a judgment that a man makes about the morality of his actions. Since one of the premises that must enter into that judgment is the teaching of the magisterium, "the 'right to form judgment of conscience' is delimited by the duty 'to adhere sincerely' to the judgments of the supreme magisterium."[57]

The bishops offer advice about how they believe a Catholic should arrive at a decision of conscience in the matter of birth control:

The Holy Father has the right given by Christ to forbid or allow a moral action. He has forbidden artificial regulation of birth. And he has done it in the most solemn way short of an infallible pronouncement. And he has not acted lightly or capriciously. And he says that what he forbids is intrinsically evil. And he has the charism of the assistance of the Holy Spirit on matters of this kind, which I do not enjoy in my private studies. And the Second Vatican Council says that I must follow his teachings. So I accept his pastoral and moral guidance.[58]

Since the majority of their people are unable to form their own consciences because of lack of education, the bishops warn priests, who may hold positions differing from the encyclical, that they are not to substitute their personal convictions for the teachings of the Holy Father.

We are not asking you to tell our people that you agree with the Holy Father if in conscience you do not. We are only asking you to teach them what the Holy Father has taught, as his teaching, not necessarily as yours. After all, it is not really proper to use the pulpit and the confessional as channels of our private feelings and personal interests.[59]

The bishops conclude their statement with the suggestion that the basic reason for opposition to *Humanae Vitae* may be traced to a total misunderstanding of the intentions of Vatican II—a misunderstanding which they describe as "a post-conciliar apostasy presented under the guise of renewal."[60]

THE FRENCH BISHOPS

The French bishops issued a pastoral note on the Pope's encyclical at the close of a plenary assembly held at Lourdes on November 2–9. Stating that they deliberately delayed their remarks in order to have time for extensive consultation with priests, theologians, and lay people, they express their intention to respond to both the desire of the Pope and to the expectations of the faithful.

They point out that in the encyclical the Pope has taken a position on a specific subject which, at his request, was not discussed at the Council. Nevertheless, the papal teaching is set within the framework of the Council's teaching on marriage as presented in *Gaudium et Spes,* and it is in this conciliar context that the Pope develops his fundamental teaching that there is "an essential link between the union of spouses and openness to the transmission of life."[61] This teaching leaves no doubt "that contraception in itself cannot be a good."[62]

Though decrying "the contraceptive mentality that has already done so much harm to France,"[63] the bishops nonetheless realize their obligation to be attentive to the sufferings of conscience experienced by those Catholics who are "divided between their will to be faithful to the teaching of the Pope and the almost insurmountable difficulties they encounter."[64] They cannot ignore, either, "the uneasiness of those who, at the conclusion of serious studies, have reached different conclusions."[65]

The bishops first address themselves to those who accept the encyclical but find themselves unable to respond to its demands. These people should not be discouraged; they should rest assured that the failings of spouses, who are otherwise generous in their personal and apostolic life, "are not of a gravity comparable to the faults of those couples who despise this teaching and allow themselves to be dominated by egotism and the search for pleasure.[66] Contraception," the bishops go on to say, "can never be a good. It is always a disorder, but this disorder is not always culpable."[67] They base this conclusion on the traditional teaching that when a conflict of duties exists, one must decide which is the greater duty. Married couples who find themselves in such a conflict situation must therefore reflect together and decide before God which duty in the circumstances is the greater.[68]

As for those who find themselves unable to accept the teaching of the encyclical, the bishops implore them not to hold their convictions as definitive, but to continue their research, to discuss the results of that research with the bishops and, above all else, to avoid polemics that trouble souls and arouse division in the Church.

The statement ends with these words. "Around love and marriage one of the decisive struggles of our time is being fought. On its outcome depend the man and the society of tomorrow."[69]

THE BISHOPS OF THE UNITED STATES[70]

On July 31, 1968, Archbishop John F. Dearden, president of the National Conference of Catholic Bishops, issued a brief statement in the name of the bishops of the United States, calling for a "true

Christian response" to *Humanae Vitae*. The encyclical reflects the constant concern of the Church for the sacredness of marriage and reaffirms the principles to be followed by married persons in the formation of their consciences.

The bishops are aware of the difficulties which this teaching entails for conscientious married people, but maintain that "we must face the reality that struggling to live out the will of God will often entail sacrifice."[71] Priests and people are solicited "to receive with sincerity" what the Pope has taught, "to study it carefully and to form their consciences in its light."[72]

When a number of theologians in Washington, D.C., of whom more will be said later, expressed their dissent from the encyclical, claiming that their stand was justified by the bishops' statement, the Most Reverend Joseph L. Bernardin, general secretary of the conference, replied that "the bishops in no way intended to imply that there is a divergence between their statement and the teaching of the Holy Father."[73]

In November, 1968, at the plenary meeting of the conference in Washington, the bishops issued an eleven-thousand-word pastoral letter discussing the problems of birth control and war. Adopted on November 15, it endorsed *Humanae Vitae* in much the same way as did the statement of July 31.

The encyclical, the bishops declare, is a positive statement concerning the nature of conjugal love and responsible parenthood. It is an obligatory statement, consistent with the moral traditions of Christian faith, as well as an authoritative statement, solemnly interpreting imperatives which are divine rather than ecclesiastical in origin. It presents without ambiguity or doubt the Church's teaching on the objective evil of contraception, and proposes a high ideal which the Church cannot compromise, even though it is difficult of attainment.

The bishops appreciate the fact that married couples are often caught in an agonizing crisis of conscience when they find it difficult to "harmonize the sexual expression of love with respect for the life-giving power of sexual union."[74] Such circumstances "may reduce moral guilt," but "no one following the teaching of the Church can deny the objective evil of contraception itself."[75] Those who have resorted to artificial contraception are urged not to become discouraged, but to continue to take advantage of the sacraments of Penance and the Eucharist.

The bishops' discussion of the question of conscience does not extend to an endorsement of the right to differ from the encyclical; it emphasizes instead the obligation of forming conscience in the light of the Church's teaching. The matter of theological dissent from non-infallible teachings is also touched upon and certain standards for such dissent indicated, i.e., the theologian must set forth his opinions with propriety, with due regard for the gravity of the subject and with proper deference to authority. His reasons must be serious and well-founded, and he must bear in mind that there is always a presumption in favor of the magisterium. If he is one who performs a pastoral ministry in the Church, he must be particularly mindful that even responsible dissent does not excuse him from the duty of faithfully presenting the authentic doctrine of the Church.

Turning their attention to priests and counsellors, the bishops earnestly ask that they heed the appeal of Pope Paul "to expound the Church's teaching on marriage without ambiguity."[76]

THE BISHOPS OF JAPAN

In a brief statement released after a meeting in Tokyo, the Japanese bishops requested Catholics to receive the encyclical in a spirit of obedience. The encyclical, they state, "deals with very important problems of the whole human race," and "defends the true values of family and society."[77]

Obedience to the Pope's teaching may create various difficulties for many husbands and wives. Yet, the bishops remind their people, married life lived in conformity to the will of God will always demand sacrifice and on this very account marriage will become "more and more fruitful." Those who try in good faith to obey the encyclical but fail in some point "because of unavoidable and objective circumstances,"[78] must not feel that they "have been separated from the love of God."[79] They should strive rather to deepen their trust in God and to participate fervently in the life of the Church and in the sacraments.

THE SWISS BISHOPS

The bishops of Switzerland, in a meeting at Solothurn, unanimously adopted a statement on the encyclical in which they said that married couples should be guided by "a safe conscience." Conscience is not autonomous, but contingent on God's will. The faithful must therefore inform their consciences with the aid of the magisterium of the Church, which is guided by the Holy Spirit. Nevertheless, the bishops, sensible of the conflicts of conscience that may arise, declare: "The faithful who cannot accept all the encyclical's instructions regarding birth control, when they are not motivated by selfishness or complacency and when honestly striving towards an ever better fulfillment of God's will, may be permitted to assume that they are not guilty before God."[80]

A COMMENT ON THE BISHOPS' STATEMENTS

The fact that there were so many statements on the encyclical by the bishops is significant. The message of *Humanae Vitae* was after all, clear and unmistakable: the prohibition of contraception was plainly reaffirmed. Why was it, then, that so many national hierarchies felt compelled to supplement it with statements of their own?

One reason is that they were asked to do so. Prior to the official release of the encyclical, the bishops received a communication from the papal secretary of state, Cardinal Cicognani, asking them to stand firm with the Pope, to present "this delicate point of the Church's teaching" and "to explain and justify the reasons for it."[81] The Holy See was cognizant, as were the bishops, of the new theological and pastoral climate in the Church that was at odds with the fundamental message of *Humanae Vitae*. In such a climate the encyclical would have difficulty in standing on its own, and only a united front on the part of the world episcopate could offer the hope of reversing the trend of thinking about birth regulation that in recent years had become more and more widespread. It was therefore out of their sense of loyalty to the Pope and their concern for unity in the Church that the bishops responded to Pope Paul's appeal for support; this, at least in part, accounts for this unprecedented number of episcopal comments on a papal document.

It is also possible, however, to see another reason why the bishops reacted in such large numbers to the encyclical. Bishops owe loyalty not only to the Pope but to their people. Many of the bishops, as evidenced by their statements, were genuinely concerned about the crises of conscience which they knew the encyclical would create. They realized that there would be both priests and lay people among the faithful who would experience great difficulty in assenting to the encyclical's teaching on birth control. They realized, too, that there would be others of the faithful who, though feeling obligated to accept the encyclical's teaching, would find themselves unable to submit to its directives.

Some of the bishops, privately at least, may have regretted the encyclical. They may have wished that the question of intervention in intercourse had been left open or at least resolved in a less definitive way. But now the encyclical was there. They could not change its content but they could, for the sake of their people who experienced serious problems of conscience, modify that content by interpretation and pastoral clarification. They could say, as the French bishops had said, that contraception is always a disorder, but that this disorder is not always guilty. Or they could call attention to the fact, as the Austrian bishops had, that the encyclical does not speak of serious sin; hence those who cannot follow its directives need not feel that their failures would necessarily separate them from the love of God. They could soften the pressures created by the encyclical and attempt to establish a sense of perspective by reminding their people, as did the Scandinavian bishops, that in today's world there is great need for concentrating on the essentials of the Gospel and that there are more important questions to be answered than how to regulate the intimate acts of marriage. Following the example of the Canadian bishops they could point out that the Church is a pilgrim Church, that unity in this pilgrim Church must not be confused with bland uniformity, and that sometimes, as often happens in the case of pilgrims, we falter in the way or even differ as to the way.

In short, if the encyclical placed a burden on Catholics which the bishops could not remove, however much some might have wished to do so, they could at least lighten that burden by filtering it through other insights and principles.

Another significant fact about the episcopal statements is that the bishops did not speak with complete unanimity. It is true that there is a common pattern in the approach to the encyclical discernible in almost all of the bishops' statements: the desire to set the decision on contraception in the context of a wider theology of marriage, the emphasis on the positive human and Christian values affirmed in the encyclical, the discussion of the authority with which the Pope spoke, the obedience due his teaching, and the effort to resolve or, in any case, to consider sympathetically the problems which the encyclical poses for married people. But within this common pattern of approach there are many shades of difference in each of the statements, and some of the differences are substantial. The statements, in fact, range from a total endorsement of the encyclical that left little or no room for dissent to a positive justification of those who feel it their right and duty to depart from the teaching of the encyclical; in between there is an emphasis on the guiltlessness, the lessened responsibility, or at least on the good will of those who dissent.

When they discuss the most crucial issue posed by the encyclical—its authority and the assent required of Catholics—the bishops are unanimous in stating the principles that govern this issue. They agree that: (1) The encyclical, though not infallible, represents the authentic teaching of the Church. (2) Catholics are required to give to the encyclical the submission of mind and will of which Vatican II speaks.[82] (3) The encyclical is an important element in the formation of Catholic conscience. But while they concur in the principles involved, they differ—at times considerably—in their understanding and application of these principles. Some of the episcopal statements, for instance, seem to blur the distinction between infallible teaching and authentic, non-infallible teaching, giving the latter, in practice, the same weight of authority as the former; other statements declare that authentic non-infallible teaching cannot claim unconditional and absolute assent and that the possibility of change in such teaching cannot, in principle, be excluded. For some bishops submission of mind and will implies an obligation so serious that failure to accept the encyclical would be grave disobedience; for others submission of mind and will means an openness and positive receptivity to the contents of the encyclical without, however, precluding the possibility of dissent. In some of the bishops' statements the issue of freedom of conscience is sidestepped and emphasis is placed instead on the obligation to form one's conscience in accordance with the papal teaching; other statements, however, openly defend the right of conscience to dissent from certain aspects of the encyclical after due study and reflection.[83]

This divergence of approach in the episcopal statements is the clearest sign that many of the bishops, however strongly they felt it their duty to support the Pope in his teaching, also recognized their responsibility to offer, in union with him, guidelines to the faithful on an issue of great importance and serious concern for the whole Church. The fact that these guidelines do not merely echo the teaching of the Pope, but express the considered thought and reflection of the bishops as they variously interpreted the papal teaching, is the best proof that collegiality, however limited, has already entered into the life-stream of the Church.

NOTES

1. Paul VI, *Humanae Vitae*, Art. 5.
2. *New York Times,* August 3, 1968.
3. *Ibid.*
4. *Op. cit.,* August 11, 1968.
5. *Ibid.*
6. N. C. News Service, September 11, 1968.
7. *Ibid.*
8. *Ibid.*
9. *Ibid.*
10. *Ibid.*
11. *Op. cit.,* September 7, 1968.
12. *Ibid.*
13. *Ibid.*
14. *Lumen Gentium,* Art. 25.
15. N. C. News Service, September 7, 1968.
16. *Ibid.*
17. *Ibid.*
18. *Op. cit.,* September 13, 1968.
19. *Ibid.*
20. *Ibid.*
21. *Op. cit.,* October 14, 1968.
22. *Ibid.*
23. *Op. cit.,* September 21, 1968.
24. *Ibid.*
25. *Op. cit.,* October 4, 1968.
26. *Ibid.*
27. *Ibid.*
28. *Ibid.*
29. *Ibid.*
30. *Op. cit.,* September 26, 1968.
31. *Ibid.*
32. *Ibid.*
33. *Ibid.*
34. *Ibid.*
35. *Op. cit.,* September 27, 1968.
36. *Ibid.*

37. *Op. cit.,* November 29, 1968.

38. Vatican II, *Gaudium et Spes,* Art. 16.

39. *The Canadian Register,* October 5, 1968.

40. *Ibid.*

41. *Ibid.*

42. *Ibid.*

43. *Ibid.*

44. *Ibid.*

45. N. C. News Service, October 11, 1968.

46. *Ibid.*

47. *Op. cit.,* October 14, 1968.

48. *Gaudium et Spes,* Arts. 50–51.

49. N. C. News Service, October 14, 1968.

50. *Ibid.*

51. *Op. cit.,* October 24, 1968.

52. *Ibid.*

53. *Ibid.*

54. *Ibid.*

55. *Op. cit.,* November 7, 1968.

56. *Ibid.*

57. *Ibid.*

58. *Ibid.*

59. *Ibid.*

60. *Ibid.*

61. *Op. cit.,* November 22, 1968.

62. *Ibid.*

63. *Ibid.*

64. *Ibid.*

65. *Ibid.*

66. *Ibid.*

67. *Ibid.*

68. This "conflict of duties" approach, which appears also in the Belgian and Canadian statements, seems to be at variance with Art. 14 of *Humanae Vitae,* which denies that the argument of the lesser evil can be used to justify intervention in intercourse.

69. N. C. News Service, November 22, 1968.

70. See Appendix II for a brief discussion of (1) the attitudes of individual members of the American hierarchy toward the encyclical, and (2) "the Bishop Shannon case."

71. *National Catholic Reporter*, August 7, 1968.

72. *Ibid*.

73. *Ibid*.

74. *New York Times*, November 16, 1968.

75. *Ibid*. (Bishop [now Cardinal] John J. Wright, chairman of the committee that drafted the pastoral letter, said at a news conference: "I cannot conceive of circumstances under which a person could use artificial contraception and not think of himself as committing a grave sin.")

76. Paul VI, *Humanae Vitae*, Art. 28.

77. N. C. News Service, December 5, 1968.

78. *Ibid*.

79. *Ibid*.

80. *Op. cit.*, December 12, 1968.

81. Hoyt, ed., *The Birth Control Debate*, p. 143.

82. Practically all of the bishops' statements cite Art. 25 of *Lumen Gentium*.

83. The bishops' statements summarized in this chapter have been presented in chronological order according to their date of publication. It would perhaps be helpful to supplement this chronological arrangement with some attempt to classify them in terms of their content.

An analysis in these terms suggests the possibility of a threefold classification: left, center and right. The term "left" is here used to designate those episcopal statements which, though not denying the obligation of a Catholic to give serious consideration to the encyclical in the formation of conscience, would nevertheless grant that after study and reflection a Catholic could dissent from the encyclical's teaching on contraception.

The term "right" is used to designate those statements which assert with scarcely any qualification that disobedience to the encyclical is seriously wrong, that conscience must be formed in accordance with the papal teaching so that for all practical purposes the decision of the Pope becomes the decision of the individual conscience.

The term "center" would include several groups: (1) those who discuss seriously the rights of conscience, and even grant the theoretical possibility of dissent, but who stop short of endorsing such dissent in practice, (2) those who advise pastoral sympathy for the dissenting faithful, but who do not go so far as to endorse such dissension, (3) those who would grant that in many cases, at least, failure to follow the directives of the encyclical would not involve serious guilt, and (4) those who would assert that circumstances may lessen the guilt involved in failure to observe the Pope's teaching. (This group is not distinguishable from the "right.")

In terms of these classifications, the bishops' statements may be roughly arranged as follows:

Left	*Center*	*Right*
Austrian	American	Ceylon
Belgian	East German	Indian
Canadian	England and Wales	Irish
Dutch	German	Mexican
French	Italian	Philippine
Scandinavian	Japanese	Scottish
	Swiss	Spanish

X THE THEOLOGIANS AND THE ENCYCLICAL

One of the tasks of the theologian in the Church is to cooperate with the magisterium in helping the faithful understand what the magisterium is teaching. In *Humanae Vitae* Pope Paul refers to this function and calls upon moral theologians to expound the Church's teaching on marriage without ambiguity. He reminds them that it is of utmost importance for peace of conscience and the unity of Christian people that in the field of morals as well as dogma "all should attend to the magisterium of the Church and all should speak the same language."[1] He makes the plea of the Apostle Paul his own when he says: "I appeal to you, brethren, by the name of our Lord Jesus Christ, that all of you agree and that there be no dissensions among you, but that you be united in the same mind and the same judgment."[2]

Many theologians were unable to respond to this plea of the Holy Father, for they found it difficult to reconcile the fundamental message of the papal teaching with the theological development that had taken place in the Church and with the way in which many married Christians were actually experiencing the reality of marriage. They therefore felt obliged to undertake what they considered yet another function of the theologian—namely, to evaluate the teaching of the magisterium in the perspective of the faith-experience of the entire Church community. They felt that they were speaking with one voice, though it differed in certain important respects from that which the Pope had used in his encyclical. They considered it their duty to speak in a voice that respectfully dissented from various elements of his teaching.

The voice of dissent came quickly—and from many quarters. It came from men of high repute in the theological community: Bernard Häring, Karl Rahner, Hans Küng, Edward Schillebeeckx, Herbert McCabe, Richard McCormick, Bernard Cooke, John Milhaven, and others. It came from the theological faculties of such Catholic institutions as Fordham University, St. Peter's College, the University of Marquette, Alma College, the Seminary of Pope John XXIII, and the Catholic University of America. In fact, the rallying point of dissent from the encyclical in the United States was around a group of theologians at the Catholic University of America.

THE WASHINGTON STATEMENT

These Washington theologians, under the leadership of Father Charles E. Curran, obtained a copy of the full text of the encyclical the very afternoon of its publication (July 29, 1968). They met immediately at Caldwell Hall—a faculty residence on the university campus—read the encyclical, analyzed its contents, and drafted a statement. They telephoned colleagues throughout the country to invite their help in the final wording of the statement, and by 3 A.M. of July 30, had obtained eighty-seven signatures. They were now prepared to present their statement at a newspaper press conference, which was held later that morning at the Mayflower Hotel in Washington, D.C.

Father Curran read the statement and a panel of theologians answered questions from the press.

The Washington statement asserts that "it is common teaching in the Church that Catholics may dissent from authoritative, non-infallible teachings of the magisterium when sufficient reasons for doing so exist."[3] Under such circumstances, dissent is, in a special way, the duty of theologians, for "Christian tradition assigns [to them] the special responsibility of evaluating and interpreting pronouncements of the magisterium in the light of the total theological data operative in each question or statement."[4]

This is a responsibility which theologians cannot shirk because history gives ample evidence that there have been occasions in the past when authoritative non-infallible statements of the magisterium have subsequently been proven inadequate or even erroneous.

An analysis of *Humanae Vitae* indicates that though many positive values of marriage are expressed in the encyclical, there are sufficient reasons for disagreeing with certain elements in it. Some of the reasons adduced by the Washington theologians are ecclesiological in character; others relate to the ethical conclusions drawn in the encyclical.

They take exception to the ecclesiology implicit in the papal teaching. It does not, they maintain, reflect the Church's authentic self-awareness expressed in and suggested by the acts of the Second Vatican Council. It consistently assumes that the Church is identical with the hierarchical office, and in the context of such an ecclesiology it fails to give sufficient weight to the witness of the total life of the Church, especially the witness of married couples. It is, moreover, insensitive to the witness of the separated Christian churches and of many men of good will.

The theologians likewise fault the encyclical on the methodology it uses to arrive at some of its specific conclusions. These conclusions, they feel, are based on a concept of natural law which competent philosophers and theologians have come to see as inadequate, for it is an understanding of natural law based on a static world-view "which downplays the historical and evolutionary character of humanity in its finite existence." It is a natural law doctrine which tends to separate human sexuality from the human person and consequently to overemphasize the biological aspects of conjugal relations as ethically normative. In this respect *Humanae Vitae* shows little advance over Pius XI's *Casti Connubii;* yet the conclusions of this latter document have been called into question for some time and for serious reasons.

In view of the total theological data existing in the Church, therefore, the theologians feel it their duty to express their minds candidly on the subject.

As Roman Catholic theologians, conscious of our duty and our limitations, we conclude that spouses may responsibly decide according to their conscience that artificial contraception in some circumstances is permissible and indeed necessary to preserve and foster the values and the sacredness of marriage.[5]

On the day following the Mayflower Hotel meeting of the theologians, Archbishop Dearden issued a statement in the name of the bishops of the United States, calling upon priests and people to receive the encyclical with sincerity, "to study it carefully and to form their consciences in its light."[6] Father Curran was quick to point out that the bishops' admonition to Catholics to form their consciences *in the light of the encyclical* implied the possibility of dissent and was therefore in substantial agreement with the statement of the theologians. Bishop Bernardin, as previously mentioned, disagreed, and in a formal statement made it clear that the bishops' statement was intended as an endorsement of the encyclical. He acknowledged that people must form their own consciences, but insisted that they also have the responsibility to form a correct conscience. In the process of doing so, they must accept the Pope's teaching with that religious submission of mind and will of which the Second Vatican Council spoke.

Subsequent to the Mayflower Hotel meeting, the Washington statement was sent to theologians and teachers of theology all over the United States. They were asked to study the statement and, if they agreed in substance with its position, to sign it. There was a strong response of approval. The list of signatures grew from eighty-seven to over six hundred.

IN SUPPORT OF THE ENCYCLICAL

Austin Vaughan

Not all theologians agreed with the Washington statement. Msgr. Austin Vaughan, president of the Catholic Theological Society, expressed his disagreement in a prepared statement. Without discussing the contraceptive issue itself, he points to the ecclesiological significance of the Pope's statement. Though granting the non-infallible character of the encyclical, he discounts as wishful thinking any expectation that there will be a change in a teaching, that had been studied for so long and that reiterates a long-standing tradition.

Since the position taken in the encyclical represents the official teaching of the Church, it demands internal assent from all Catholics, including moral theologians. To withhold this assent is to call into question the magisterium itself and what it represents, for it is through the magisterium that the Holy Spirit sheds light on revelation or on human life, or on some aspect of either.

Msgr. Vaughan goes on:

I do not think it possible that what has been laid down in this document could be anything else than what the Holy Spirit, who guides our use of our resources with his providence, wants and expects of us as Catholics at this moment in the plan of salvation, apart from what direction the course of that plan might take in the future. If it were, the guidance of the Holy Spirit, promised to the magisterium according to the Constitution on the Church, would be an illusion.[7]

As for the rights of conscience, Msgr. Vaughan admits that every man must follow his conscience. Nevertheless, he maintains that acceptance of Catholic faith involves "acceptance of the guidance of the Church as an obligatory way of forming his conscience,"[8] where such guidance is provided; and it was the precise purpose of the encyclical to provide this guidance.

Theologians who wish to work for a future change in this teaching can do so, not by denying the teaching, but by asking vital questions regarding its meaning, by posing objections, by seeking a deeper understanding, and by remaining open to additional information that might throw new light on the subject.

Charles R. Meyer

Rev. Charles R. Meyer, professor of theology at St. Mary of the Lake Seminary, Mundelein, Illinois, offers a detailed critique of the Washington theologians' statement. Citing a number of objections to the encyclical that were made in their statement, Father Meyer denies validity to all of them.

Some of the objections, he says, are unworthy of the learned theologians who propose them. One, for example, is their suggestion that the encyclical consistently identifies the Church with its hierarchical office. To offer this as an objection to the encyclical is simply to ignore the fact that from earliest times it had been customary to use the word "Church" to designate not just the whole body of the faithful, but any identifiable segment of it.

Other objections, he claims, involve a misreading or a misinterpretation of the Pope's words. To say that the papal document ignores the witness of the whole Church and of other men of good will is to take no cognizance of the contrary witness of countless members of the Church who, at great sacrifice to themselves, continue to observe the traditional norms. In fact, it was precisely this double witness in the Church that created a state of doubt which could be resolved only by an authoritative statement.

It is also a misreading of the encyclical to say that the Pope absolutized a particular theory of natural law. On the contrary, the Pope, without necessarily committing the Church to a particular understanding of natural law, simply resolved the confusion arising from a plurality of natural law theories by setting forth as a practical norm for action that theory of natural law which has been traditionally and consistently supported by both theologians and the magisterium down through the ages.

It is not fair to say, either, that the encyclical places too much emphasis on the biological aspects of conjugal relations as ethically normative. The encyclical clearly recognizes the unitive aspect of the marital act; it simply refuses to separate the unitive meaning of that act from its procreative purpose. This position taken in the encyclical is fully justified by the fact that those who defended the separability of these two aspects of intercourse have simply been unable to offer convincing proof of that separability.

At the close of his article, Father Meyer makes it clear that what prompts him to reject the Washington theologians' statement is not primarily his disagreement with the objections they raise to the teaching of the encyclical, but his inability to accept the conclusion which they draw. He maintains that even if these objections were totally valid, there still would be no justification for the judgment that Catholics may decide that contraception in certain circumstances may be necessary in marriage. He denies that Catholics may dissent from non-infallible teachings, even when reasons for doing so may seem to exist. Dissent is not the prerogative of every Catholic, but only of those who are experts. Even those who qualify as experts may not withhold their assent in every instance, but only in those situations where they are proposing "to the proper authorities reasons which have not yet been considered by the magisterium in reaching its decision."[9]

Anthony T. Padovano

Father Anthony T. Padovano, professor of theology at Immaculate Conception Seminary in Darlington, New Jersey, addressed three hundred priests of the Newark archdiocese who had gathered in September, 1968, to discuss *Humanae Vitae* and the statement of dissent of the Washington theologians.

Father Padovano said that he supported *Humanae Vitae* without qualification, affirmed its contents, and accepted its enduring validity. He deplored the fact that only one side of the theological community had been heard since the publication of the encyclical, and was firm in his opinion that those who supported the encyclical should also be given a hearing.

In his talk he discusses the status of the encyclical in the Church in terms of the authority it bears, the care with which it was composed, and the way in which it has been received in the Church.

The encyclical carries with it the authority of the Vicar of Christ; Pope Paul had issued his carefully prepared decision in the strongest manner possible short of a definition, and he had not spoken until he had listened to all sides of the question. When he finally did speak, his statement did not ignore the opinions of those who advocated change in the Church's teaching on contraception; rather, it disagreed with them after they had been heard. If the Pope had not consulted them, "he would have acted less honorably than he did." If he had bound himself to follow the majority opinion of the papal commission, he would have "lacked courage and have denied the Church the unique witness of his office."[10] And even though he rejected the commission's majority opinion, Pope Paul did not stand alone in the teaching he proposed. Both before and since its publication, the overwhelming majority of the worldwide episcopate gave their approval to what he taught.[11]

The primary question for priests, Father Padovano insists, should not concern their acceptance or rejection of the encyclical, for "history is against those who resist the papacy and the episcopate in a matter of such urgency and solemnity, a matter so intimately united with conscience and the nature of Christian marriage."[12]

The main question that priests must face is, What are they going to do for their people? If by preaching and counseling they lead their people to neglect or ignore the encyclical, they are betraying their priestly ministry; at the same time they are taking a stand that is doomed to ultimate failure because "the laity will not long abide . . .

open defiance of the papacy and the bishops. Many will listen; some will applaud; but the vast majority will stand with Paul."[13]

While holding firm to the teaching of the encyclical, priests must proclaim the Church's teaching with compassion. The Church denounces errors, not persons. Pope Paul has indicated what is sinful; he has not said who is a sinner. Only God can judge whether those who practice artificial birth control are guilty of serious sin or whether, for any number of reasons, their moral guilt may be diminished. "It is one thing to say *something* is seriously wrong; it is quite another to say *some one* is seriously wrong."[14]

Priests who attempt a tyrannical enforcement of the encyclical which shows no regard for the weakness of people, are just as wrong in their own way as those who reject the encyclical outright. "Those who showed no love for people before this encyclical was issued have no business waving it before them now."[15]

Lawrence L. McReavy

Theologians who defend the encyclical tend to emphasize its authority rather than its content. A different approach, however, is taken by the moral theologian, Father Lawrence L. McReavy. He accepts the authority of the encyclical without qualification because it comes from the Vicar of Christ who in a special way enjoys the guidance of the Holy Spirit. But, in an article published in the *Clergy Review,* Father McReavy gives particular emphasis to the content of the papal document, especially to what he calls "its essential doctrine." He takes issue with those critics of the encyclical who "cavalierly" dismiss its interpretation of the natural law as "a mere exercise of natural reasoning." This, he insists, is precisely what the encyclical is not intended to be, namely, an interpretation of natural law in the light of human reason alone. The Holy Father is careful to emphasize that the doctrine he presents is derived not from natural reason alone, but from natural reason illuminated and enriched by divine revelation.

Man's moral conduct cannot be judged adequately from just the perspective of nature. Only an integral view of man—which includes an understanding of his supernatural vocation—can do justice to the moral imperatives that govern his life. "The revealed truth of man's supernatural and eternal vocation is . . . a factor of cardinal importance in judging how he is to exercise his sexual faculty in his present temporal situation."[16]

Right reason, on its own, can discern a twofold significance in the conjugal act: its procreative orientation and its unitive purpose. It can see in them evidence of the will of the Creator which man must respect, but that is as far as human reason, unaided, can go. When faced with the question, Must both these values be preserved in every case, or can one be sacrificed to preserve the other? human reason falters. It is precisely at this point that it becomes necessary to approach the problem in the revealed light of man's supernatural and eternal vocation.

Revelation makes it clear that human sexuality and its exercise in marriage involve more than a natural function directed to the perpetuation of human life on earth and the fulfillment of man and woman in unitive love. Revelation confronts us with the mystery of divine love, which calls men to be collaborators in building up the Kingdom of God and the household of the Heavenly Father where men will live with Him in eternal union and love. God wills the creation of an immortal soul when a man and a woman by the free exercise of their sexuality bring about the conception of a new entity.

Seen in this perspective, the procreative orientation of the conjugal act "acquires a sacredness which no amount of natural reasoning could ever discern."[17]

Because of this sacredness attached to human sexuality, one can understand why Christian faith has always ascribed extraordinary value to the virtue of chastity. It is in this light—coming only from revelation—that it is possible to see why husbands and wives "are morally bound to respect the procreative no less than the unitive sig-

nificance of the conjugal act whenever they choose to engage in it."
Hence:

To use [the conjugal act] as an expression of love and yet deprive it of
its lifeward direction by deliberate interference with the natural processes
which precede, accompany, and follow it, is to gainsay the loving design and invitation of the life-giving God. It is to treat as belonging exclusively to the couple a faculty which was designed to associate them
intimately and to a unique degree with the universal Father.[18]

JOHN J. O'CALLAGHAN

In a thoughtful article offering reflections on *Humanae Vitae*, John
J. O'Callaghan, S.J., professor of moral theology at the Bellarmine
School of Theology, North Aurora, Illinois, takes what might be
called a moderate stand on the encyclical which, while not completely
supporting the papal statement, yet falls short of dissenting from it.
He rejects at the outset what he considers two extreme views: the one
claiming that *Humanae Vitae* closed the door to all further discussion and the other suggesting that educated Catholics should
simply ignore the encyclical. At the same time he praises the balanced
reaction of the Washington theologians, and others like them, who
gave "respectful attention to what the encyclical said—but not un-
critical attention."[19] This seems to him a responsible theological
stance, for though "the presumption of truth" belongs to the
magisterium, this presumption must yield to opposing reasons that
are overwhelmingly clear. Those who feel that such reasons exist are
not only allowed to dissent, they may well be under an obligation to
do so.

Although conceding the right of dissent to those who are firmly
convinced of the inadequacy of *Humanae Vitae's* position, Father
O'Callahan writes principally for those who, like himself, still remain in a state of doubt—not totally convinced of the encyclical's reasoning; not totally convinced of the opposite views either.

He suggests, as his own point of view, that the encyclical may be providing for the Church not new knowledge, but an important "value-emphasis." He asks: "Is it possible that what Pope Paul is affirming in *Humanae Vitae* is a very true and necessary value-emphasis, which is valid quite independently of the reasons he gives?"[20]

Recent historical studies, he continues, have clearly shown that the Church in her teaching on marriage has constantly defended the central thesis of the *bonum matrimonii et prolis* and stressed the peripheral thesis of the *malum contraceptionis* only periodically—at those junctures of history, that is, when the peripheral thesis was necessary to the central thesis. "Is it possible that this is one of those junctures and that this consideration gives a validity to the encyclical's absolute ban on artificial contraception which an abstract "natural law" argumentation cannot?"[21]

Father O'Callaghan offers as an analogy the post-Tridentine de-emphasis on private scripture reading. He notes that scripture scholars today are stressing the fact that the Bible is essentially a liturgical book intended for community reading and its proper meaning is understood only in the context of the community. It may be, he suggests, that the discouragement in the post-Tridentine Church of private Bible reading actually involved a value-emphasis, imperfectly understood at the time but touching upon a deeper truth that we are only now beginning to understand.

Speaking of the pastoral approach to the problem of contraception, Father O'Callaghan indicates how his own thinking has changed in the light of the encyclical. He would "no longer recommend artificial birth control as something indifferent, dependent for its goodness or badness upon the generosity or selfishness of the procreative attitude operative in the marriage as a whole."[22] Rather, he would try to communicate to penitents the value-emphasis of the encyclical, proposing an *ideal* of conjugal chastity that would exclude contraception. At the same time he would explain that he was doing so on the basis of "not intrinsic reasons, but extrinsic presumption about the magisterium in the absence of totally convincing opposite arguments."[23]

If penitents accept this value-emphasis as correct yet cannot give up contraception, he would not judge them *a priori* as guilty of serious sin. Conversely, if they cannot see the Pope's value-emphasis, but are good people with otherwise correct values, he says:

I could not rule out "invincible ignorance" at the very least or even that studied conviction to which a presumption of correctness in fallible teaching must yield . . . [after all] I could not and do not judge Bernard Häring guilty of sinful imprudence in disagreeing with the encyclical; why should I so judge some one else who has thought, prayed and anguished over it? As *America* magazine for August 17 put it so well: "The abdication of personal moral responsibility has never been a doctrine of the Church."[24]

RICHARD A. McCORMICK

In *Theological Studies'* "Notes on Moral Theology" for December, 1968, Father Richard A. McCormick offers some perceptive reflections on the problem of assent and dissent in the Church with regard to authentic, non-infallible teachings of the magisterium. He applies his reflections to the debate started by *Humanae Vitae*.

Working from the commonly accepted principle that the privileged position of the magisterium generates a presumption that its teaching is correct, McCormick asks what the mental stance of a Catholic should be in the face of such a presumption. For answer, he offers the suggestion that it would be well to move away from the "vocabulary of conformity" which for so long has dominated discussions about the non-infallible magisterium. This vocabulary expresses itself in such juridical terms as "the binding force of the encyclical" or the duty to obey its teaching." It would be better, he believes, to think of the authentic teaching of the magisterium as a gift offered to the Christian community. The normal reaction to a gift is a willingness to be the recipient of it. This, in turn, is usually followed by grateful acceptance; but, in rare cases, there may be serious reasons for refusing the gift that is proffered.

In the light of this analogy, the immediate response to an authentic teaching seen as a gift is the will to assent, which normally issues in actual assent. Assent, however, cannot be immediate because it involves an act of personal appropriation which requires time and reflection. When presented with the gift of authentic, non-infallible teaching, therefore, the proper frame of mind for a Catholic should be a strong inclination to accept and assimilate the teaching and to make it one's own.

Such an inclination would presuppose a number of mental attitudes: (1) respect for the magisterial authority and an openness to its teaching, (2) a readiness to reassess one's own thinking in the light of that teaching, (3) a reluctance to conclude that the teaching of the magisterium is erroneous, even when the evidence supporting it seems to be inadequate, and (4) the adoption of a style of external behavior which shows respect and support for the magisterium.

In most cases such a mentality will result in actual assent to the magisterium's teaching; but this will not necessarily be so in every case because the genuine will to accept authentic teaching does not absolve a person, particularly a theologian, from the responsibility of submitting that teaching to methodical inquiry. Such an inquiry might lead him, despite his strong inclination to do otherwise, to voice his dissent. Normally this would happen only after some time had elapsed, for it would take a while to carry out the inquiry. In the case of *Humanae Vitae,* if the reaction of dissent came much more quickly than might decently be expected, it was simply due to the rather exceptional circumstance that the teaching expressed in the encyclical had already been submitted to such inquiry for a number of years.

Under what circumstances could methodical inquiry into a particular teaching lead to legitimate dissent? Would such dissent, for example, be warranted in the case of an individual theologian who, after serious study, finds himself personally unable to justify a particular non-infallible teaching? Father McCormick is of the opinion that in such an instance the presumption supporting the teaching would still prevail, "until a sufficient number of mature and well-informed members of the community shared this same difficulty."[25] Until such a stage is reached, an individual's difficulties, instead of starting him down the road to disagreement, may well suggest to him his own limitations. "But once it becomes clear that a large number of loyal, docile and expert Catholics share this same difficulty, then it would seem that the presumption supporting the certain correctness of the teaching would be weakened, at least to the extent that the doctrine could be said to be doubtful."[26]

If the presumption would not be weakened in such a situation, asks Father McCormick, when would it ever be? Once this point was reached, than "one would wonder whether such a doctrine could give rise to a certain obligation in conscience."[27]

In applying his reflections to *Humanae Vitae's* teaching that contraception is intrinsically evil and always illicit, McCormick makes three points:

1. Before the publication of *Humanae Vitae,* a good number of theologians, after literally thousands of hours of study and discussion, had reached the conclusion that the norms on birth control laid down by Pius XI and Pius XII were genuinely doubtful, i.e., there were serious and positive reasons for questioning these norms.

2. The publication of *Humanae Vitae* has failed to resolve the problem. It has added another authoritative voice, but no new argumentation. The vast majority of theologians, Father McCormick believes, will continue to apply to *Humanae Vitae* the same objections they had with *Casti Connubii.* They will conclude that the line of argumentation is based on an unacceptable identification of natural law with natural processes.

3. Following the publication of *Humanae Vitae,* theologians may be moved, out of a spirit of docility to the magisterium, to seek other possible grounds for establishing the intrinsic immorality of contraception. But the probability of success in such a venture is highly questionable. Serious and arduous efforts in this direction over the past several years have not only failed, but have pointed up all the

more sharply the fact that there appears to be no argument capable of sustaining the thesis that contraception is intrinsically evil; if anything, there seems to be a good deal of evidence for denying this thesis.

In the light of these reflections, Father McCormick expresses the following opinion:

The intrinsic immorality of every contraceptive act remains a teaching subject to solid and positive doubt. This is not to say that this teaching of *Humanae Vitae* is certainly erroneous. It is only to say that there are very strong objections that can be urged against it and very little evidence that will sustain it. One draws this conclusion reluctantly and with no small measure of personal anguish.[28]

What remains, then, of the presumption in favor of the correctness of the magisterium's teaching? Does this presumption still prevail? Father McCormick's answer is this:

If other theologians, after meticulous research and sober reflection, share this opinion in sufficient numbers, if bishops and competent married couples would arrive at the same conclusion, it is difficult to see how the teaching would not lose the presumption of certainty ordinarily enjoyed by authoritative utterances.[29]

Father McCormick concludes with some tentative pastoral suggestions for bishops and priests. The responsibility of bishops, as true teachers in the Church, is not discharged simply by the decision "to support the Pope." Such a decision is no more than a "policy decision" and fails to indicate whether the bishops are truly accepting and teaching a doctrine, or simply enforcing it. The teaching charism which the bishops are called upon to exercise in the Church demands of them a truly personal reflection that will offer positive guidance to the faithful. There is a difference between "accepting the authority of the Pope" and "accepting what is authoritatively taught."

In dealing with priests, the bishops have a right to insist on a genuine Christian docility to the Pope and his teaching office, and the need on the part of priests for serious study, reflection, and consultation. It would be a mistake, however, for bishops to insist on assent from their priests. "We shall only grow in knowledge and understanding in the Catholic community if acceptance of this or any teaching is completely uncoerced and if it represents, as far as possible, a truly personal assimilation, even though this assimilation may be somewhat delayed."[30]

Priests, in their dealings with the faithful, must take care to distinguish between their own personal opinion and authoritative teaching. They must help the faithful to personal reflection and assimilation of the encyclical, especially its positive values. They should not attempt to mold the consciences of the faithful, but rather help them to form their own.

Dissent from the teaching on contraception should not constitute a reason for denying absolution in the sacrament of Penance. In the case of reflective and competent married people who dissent from this teaching, their decision should be respected.

The most difficult pastoral problem concerns those married couples who are incapable of making a personal, evaluative judgment. If they are trying to live their married lives responsibly in terms of values stated in *Humanae Vitae,* "a strong case can be made for saying that their individual acts of contraception should not be viewed by them or judged by the confessor to be subjectively serious sin."[31]

KARL RAHNER

In a rather long article in the September, 1968, issue of *Stimmen der Zeit,* Karl Rahner, without taking a stand on the substantive content of the encyclical (which he says would require a much lengthier study), addresses himself to two problems: (1) the theological significance of the disagreement existing in the Church in the aftermath of the encyclical, and (2) the line of conduct appropriate for various groups in the Church in the light of this undeniable diversity of opinion.

He discusses the place and purpose in the Church of authentic, non-defined teaching. Such teaching is necessary because the Church is often faced with questions in the realm of faith and morals that simply cannot be resolved in an either-or fashion—either by making an infallible decision or by simply leaving the matter to the arbitrary opinion of the individual. Of such a situation, he says:

> For the sake of protecting its own ultimate substance of faith, the Church must, despite the danger of an error in the individual case, express doctrinal instructions which have a definite degree of binding force and still, because not a definition of faith, bear in themselves a certain provisional quality as far as the possibility of error is concerned.[32]

Teachings of this kind, representing "the best knowledge and conscience" of the Church authority at the time, carry with them a presumption in favor of their objective correctness. However, because they are at the same time "temporary doctrinal expressions" based on fallible insights, they are basically capable of reform. Catholics, therefore, "have both the right and the responsibility to count on the possibility of reform of a Church document which does not present any definition."[33] In other words, the presumption favoring the correctness of a magisterial teaching does not eliminate the contrary presumption of the possibility of review and subsequent reform of that teaching.

In the light of this twofold presumption generated by a teaching that is authentic but not definitive or irreformable, it is entirely possible that a Catholic conscience can arrive at the conviction that it is not bound by a particular teaching. This is especially understandable in those instances where the magisterium has not succeeded in making comprehensible the actual justification of its teaching, and even more so when there appear to be formidable reasons for nonacceptance.

Applying these general ideas to *Humanae Vitae,* Father Rahner observes that the encyclical "will not prove psychologically effective with many people."[34] First of all, the document is too brief to be genuinely persuasive. Secondly, its intrinsic argumentation is far from convincing. It adopts a closed and static view of human nature that leaves little room for free and responsible decision. Its attempt to justify rhythm, while forbidding all other methods of birth regulations, will be regarded by many as subtle hairsplitting. Thirdly, a notable majority of the papal commission members, including theologians and bishops, spoke against the position subsequently adopted in the encyclical. This generally known fact will make it extremely difficult for many Catholics to convince themselves of the soundness of the papal stand.

In view of these psychological factors—and quite apart from the question of whether or not they are objectively valid—the conclusion must be drawn that "the actual situation with regard to the mentality and the life-practice of the majority of Catholics after the encyclical will not be changed."[35] In fact, Rahner suggests, the numerous protests that have already arisen in the Church indicate that "for the majority of Catholics the norm of the encyclical will practically be considered not only as a *doctrina reformabilis,* but also as a *doctrina reformanda.*"[36] In the face of so widespread an attitude in the Church, one is justified in making the theological judgment that—and again, apart from the objective reasons which may or may not warrant such an attitude—"the *bona fides* of a subjectively innocent conscience cannot be denied."[37]

Appropriate Conduct in the Church

In the remainder of his article, Rahner addresses himself to the second problem. In the light of the foregoing theological judgment, what should be the appropriate line of conduct for bishops, priests, theologians, and married couples?

Bishops, without prejudice to their personal convictions about the papal ruling, have the responsibility of pointing out the importance of the encyclical and the duty on the part of the faithful to give it serious consideration. They must especially caution against any emotional and unreflective reactions that would make light of the Church's teaching authority. On the other hand, however, it would be wrong for the bishops to act "as if the papal declaration were simply incapable of reform and as if any dissenting from it would necessarily imply a basic denial of the Church's teaching authority."[38] It would be equally wrong for them to attempt to stifle open discussion of the papal teaching or to impose ecclesiastical sanctions on priests who discreetly and respectfully propose another point of view.

Priests, in counselling the faithful, should emphasize the positive and undisputed elements of Catholic teaching and not allow themselves to be drawn into a position where it would appear that the only significant question of marriage morality is whether one is for or against the pill. They should not attempt to "enlighten" the consciences of those who accept the papal teaching, but neither should they upset the good faith of those who in good conscience dissent from that teaching.

Loyalty to the magisterium requires that the moral theologian communicate to his listeners the teaching of the encyclical and the basic reasons behind the papal position. He must not feel, however, that he has no other choice but to defend the encyclical from every conceivable point of view, or to keep silent. On the contrary, it is his duty to present both sides of the question. To defend the encyclical as absolutely certain would be to sacrifice the credibility of his position as a theologian, for it is impossible to ignore "the objectively present and subjectively very effective difficulties" that run counter to the papal teaching; on the other hand, to remain silent in such a situation would be to abdicate his responsibility as a theologian. Indeed, if the theologian did not feel free and if, actually, he were not free to express his dissent from reformable teachings when he had reasons for such dissent, it is difficult to see how development and correction of the Church's official teaching could ever take place.

Married Catholics who, after full reflection and honest self-criticism, have arrived at a position which departs from the papal norm, need not feel that they are subjectively guilty or formally disobedient to the authority of the Church. They should not feel, either, that once they have made an earnest judgment of conscience that they have to put this judgment to the test each time they receive the sacrament of Penance. At the same time their love and loyalty should move them to avoid destructive criticism and "wild recriminations" against the Church.

Doctrinal Development

Father Rahner concludes with a word on the necessity of openness to doctrinal development within the Church. He says:

Whatever might have taken place psychologically in the consciousness of the average Catholic in his relationship to the Church, especially in the last one hundred years, it is not true that the Catholic Church has understood or still understands itself as a church in which everything important is immediately clear and in its absolute possession, and that the discovery of truth takes place purely and simply through the pronouncements of its highest teaching office.[39]

The magisterium of the Church is an indispensable element in the discovery of truth and the development of doctrine, but it is not the only element. Other factors—such as the "sense" of the faithful, new insights of individual Christians and theologians, new situations that pose new questions—also contribute to the clarification of the faith-consciousness of the Church and its doctrinal development. It should be clear that "the authority of the magisterium in the Church and its respectability do not demand that a person act in the Church as if all theological positions in the Church are only the obedient repetition of a declaration of this magisterium."[40]

BERNARD HÄRING

The most noted theologian among the original eighty-seven signers of the Washington statement was Bernard Häring, the German theologian whose three-volume *Law of Christ* has already become a contemporary classic in Catholic moral theology. The evening before the meeting at the Mayflower Hotel, Father Charles E. Curran, who had studied under Father Häring in Rome, contacted his former teacher by telephone (Häring was lecturing at Santa Barbara, California, at the time) and asked for his support. "I almost fell off the chair when he said Yes," Curran said.[41]

Father Häring's decision to add his name to the list of dissenting theologians was significant, not only because of the worldwide respect he enjoys as a moral theologian, but for two additional reasons. First, he had been secretary of Vatican II's subcommission on marriage and the family, and a member of the theological section of the papal birth commission. Secondly, up to the time of the encyclical's publication, he had exercised great caution concerning the birth control issue and had not really taken an unambiguous stand. His support, then, of the Washington statement could be expected to carry considerable weight in the theological community.

Father Häring gave the reasons for his decision in a statement issued to the *National Catholic Reporter*. For one thing he is acting out of loyalty to the Church and especially to the Pope. He says: "If only our own personal convictions would be at stake, reverence and love toward the Holy Father would be a sufficient motive for me to be silent forever."[42]

Loyalty to the Church, however, demands a total dedication to the whole people of God, and the absolute and unambiguous wording of the encyclical—allowing of no exceptions even when the mental health of a person or the stability of a marriage is at stake—places an intolerable burden on many people, particularly the poor, the uneducated, and the scrupulous about whom he is very concerned.

Loyalty to the Church also requires concern for its credibility. The encyclical has shaken the faith and trust of many, for by absolutizing biological processes it seems to disassociate the Church from modern medicine and modern culture. Biological processes are certainly a part of the human person, yet "the biological realities must serve the wholeness of the person, and the whole person must not be submitted to biological processes if these would destroy the person."[43]

If the Church wishes to speak in a credible way about natural law to the world at large and to modern people within the Church, then it must show that natural law by definition "is based on human experience, reflection, insights and convincing arguments."[44] The encyclical, by and large, has failed to do this.

Father Häring expresses the conviction that the position taken in the encyclical could not be the last word of the Catholic Church on the subject of birth regulation; he therefore appeals to the Holy Father to use all the resources of collegiality in order to come to a broader consensus of opinion and to reach a solution worked out by the whole Christian community.

Meanwhile, he voices the hope that the crisis created by *Humanae Vitae* will not lead to panic in the Church. It would be absurd, he says, to think that a person must leave the Church or renounce his loyalty to the Pope because he is unable to accept the encyclical's teaching. A readiness to learn from the magisterium, even when it does not speak infallibly, is a fundamental stance in the life of a Christian; at the same time it is equally fundamental to the life of the Christian community that the teaching of the magisterium should not be isolated from the knowledge and faith of the whole Church.

On the question of whether the encyclical binds the consciences of all Catholics, Father Häring offers the following observations:

1. Those who are able to accept the encyclical with an honest conscience must do so.

2. Those who are in doubt as to whether or not they can accept the encyclical's teaching must study that teaching thoroughly and consult other informed sources, in order to clarify their consciences.

3. Those who cannot accept the ruling of the encyclical and who dissent with an honest and informed conscience, must follow their sincere conviction. Married couples who, for good reasons and with a sincere conscience, make responsible use of those methods of birth control which they consider best can do so without incurring guilt.

4. Priests must inform the faithful of the Pope's teaching without, however, feeling obliged to present *Humanae Vitae* as the final word of the Church.[45]

GREGORY BAUM

Few theologians have been so outspoken in their call for revision of the Church's teaching on birth control as the colorful and sometimes controversial Augustinian priest, Father Gregory Baum. As early as 1965, in anticipation of a papal statement on the birth control issue, he had expressed his opinion on the meaning that such a statement would have for the Catholic Church: It would offer valuable and important guidance for the formation of a Catholic's conscience, but it would not settle the matter once and for all. In an article written in December of that same year, reporting on the Council and detailing the last minute efforts of the papal secretary of state to include a condemnation of birth control in the Council's statement on marriage and the family, Father Baum had written:

Since the conscience of the Church is so deeply divided on this issue and since the solution is in no way contained in divine revelation, the authoritative norms which the Pope himself, as universal teacher, will propose in due time, shall not be a definitive interpretation of divine law, binding under all circumstances, but rather offer an indispensable and precious guide for the Christian conscience.[46]

According to Baum, the solution to the problem of the morality of birth control is nowhere to be found in divine revelation. Whatever can be said about birth control morality belongs rather to that area of natural wisdom, or understanding of human morality, that has customarily been called the natural law.

Does the Church have the authority to teach in this area of natural wisdom? Father Baum contends that it does. He points out, however, that this is not the primary and central object of the Church's teaching office. The magisterium exists primarily to teach divine revelation, namely, what Jesus taught us to believe (faith) and what He taught us to do (morals). It is in this area of divine revelation, and in this area alone, that the Church can claim to teach with the infallible assistance of the Holy Spirit. When She teaches in any other area (e.g., the area of human morality), her teaching, though authoritative, is by its very nature non-infallible and changeable. In other words, it is fallible, which means that "at times it can even be wrong. . . . Catholics believe that since the ecclesiastical magisterium is guided by the Holy Spirit, this will not happen very often. But there is nothing in Catholic dogma to assure them that it could not occasionally happen."[47]

Indeed, history is witness to the fact that there have been occasions when the magisterium has been proved wrong. Father Baum cites as an example the principle of religious liberty, which was repeatedly condemned in papal encyclicals and other ecclesiastical documents in the nineteenth century; yet at Vatican II, it was "finally acknowledged as the new official teaching of the Church."[48]

Despite the occasional erroneous teachings of the magisterium, Catholics, because they believe that the Church does have authority to teach in the area of human wisdom, will receive the official Church teaching with gratitude and a willingness to be taught and guided by that teaching. Nevertheless, the assent which a Catholic gives to such authentic, non-infallible teaching is not absolute but conditional. It may happen, therefore, that a Catholic will be unable to assimilate a particular official teaching because it goes counter to his own rational and objective reasoning. In a situation of this kind, "a loyal Catholic may licitly dissent from an official ecclesiastical position."[49]

Father Baum offers several reasons why a Catholic might feel it necessary to dissent from the encyclical's position that contraception is always immoral.

1. The encyclical bases its condemnation of contraception on the natural law. A Catholic, whose understanding of natural law is that it is founded on the universal moral experience of mankind, may

question why, in our culture, the natural law ban on contraception would be known only by the Catholic Church. He may be reluctant to draw the conclusion that "the consciences of other men and even other Churches are so corrupt that they are no longer in touch with the foundation of human morality!"[50]

2. The word "natural" seems to be used equivocally in the encyclical. At times it refers to that which belongs to the basic structure of human life. In this sense, "nature" as a norm of morality would be man's fidelity to what he is and what he can be, and to act against nature would be to damage man's integrity as man. Again, the word "natural" is used in the encyclical to refer to the biological processes in man. Thus when *Humanae Vitae* condemns the pill and approves rhythm, it maintains that the pill, unlike rhythm, interferes with the natural processes of human life and is therefore against nature. Many will find it difficult "to explain why what is against 'nature' in a biological sense should necessarily be against 'nature' in the more profound sense of man's basic structure."[51]

3. The encyclical's argument against contraception appears to move too uncritically from the fundamental principle it enunciates to a particular application of that principle. The fundamental principle affirmed in the encyclical is that there is an inseparable unity between love and fertility in human sexuality. No theologian in the Church has ever questioned this principle; it is one that belongs to the very structure of man's historical existence. But in recent years many theologians have become convinced that this principle applies to the overall orientation of a marriage and not necessarily to every single act of intercourse. Indeed, it would seem that this was implicitly acknowledged when the Church approved the use of the rhythm method of birth control. The encyclical, however, rejects this point of view, insisting that this fundamental principle of the inseparability of love and fertility in marriage must be applied to every act of sexual union. Many Catholics will experience serious difficulties in following the line of reasoning by which the encyclical attempts to justify this position.

Catholics, Father Baum says in closing, are not rebels. They willingly acknowledge the Church's authority to teach in the areas of divine revelation, human wisdom, and rational morality. They are loyal to the Pope and want to be docile to his teaching. And this general attitude of loyalty and docility is not incompatible with dissent from a particular non-infallible teaching, when that dissent is based on objective and tested reasons.

This chapter has attempted to analyze in some detail the reactions of certain theologians to *Humanae Vitae*. In order to keep the chapter within reasonable proportions, it was necessary to restrict the number of theologians whose views were discussed. It is hoped, however, that the writings which were selected for analysis are sufficiently representative of the ongoing thinking in the theological community to be considered typical.

It should be said that it was much easier to find theologians who, in varying degrees, dissented from the encyclical's decision than it was to find those who gave it their unqualified support. This fact may well be regarded as a theological datum that is deserving of reflection within the whole community of the Church.

NOTES

1. Paul VI, *Humanae Vitae*, Art. 28.

2. *1 Cor.* 1:10.

3. "Text of the Statement by Theologians," *New York Times*, July 31, 1968.

4. *Ibid.*

5. *Ibid.*

6. *National Catholic Reporter*, August 7, 1968.

7. Austin Vaughan, statement in the *National Catholic Reporter*, August 7, 1968.

8. *Ibid.*

9. Charles R. Meyer, in Hoyt, *The Birth Control Debate*, p. 197.

10. Anthony T. Padovano, "In Defense of the Encyclical," *Catholic World* 208 (December, 1968), p. 113.

11. Father Padovano's talk was given before many of the national hierarchies had expressed their views on the encyclical. As has been indicated in the previous chapter, a number of the national hierarchies appear to be closer in their position to the statement of the Washington theologians than Father Padovano seems to have anticipated when he spoke.

12. Padovano, *op. cit.*, p. 116.

13. *Op. cit.*, p. 114

14. *Ibid.*

15. *Ibid.*

16. Lawrence L. McReavy, "The Essential Doctrine of *Humanae Vitae*," *Clergy Review* 53 (November, 1968), p. 863.

17. *Op. cit.*, p. 865.

18. *Op. cit.*, p. 866.

19. John J. O'Callaghan, "Reflections on *Humanae Vitae*," *Theology Digest* 16 (Winter, 1968), p. 318.

20. *Op. cit.*, p. 324.

21. *Ibid.*

22. *Op. cit.*, p. 327.

23. *Ibid.*

24. *Ibid.*

25. Richard A. McCormick, "Notes on Moral Theology," *Theological Studies* 29 (December, 1968), p. 732.

26. *Ibid.*

27. *Ibid.*

28. *Op. cit.*, p. 737.

29. *Op. cit.*, p. 738.

30. *Op. cit.*, p. 739.

31. *Op. cit.*, p. 741.

32. Karl Rahner, "On the Encyclical, *Humanae Vitae*," *National Catholic Reporter*, September 18, 1968. Translation by David E. Schlaver of the article in *Stimmen der Zeit*, September, 1968.

33. *Ibid.*

34. *Ibid.*

35. *Ibid.*

36. *Ibid.*

37. *Ibid.*

38. *Ibid.*

39. *Ibid.*

40. *Ibid.*

41. *National Catholic Reporter*, August 7, 1968.

42. Bernard Häring, statement in the *National Catholic Reporter*, August 7, 1968.

43. *Ibid.*

44. *Ibid.*

45. "Father Häring on the Encyclical," *London Tablet*, September 21, 1968.

46. Gregory Baum, "Birth Control—What Happened?" *Commonweal* 83 (December 24, 1965), p. 371.

47. Gregory Baum, "The Right to Dissent," *Commonweal* 88, (August 23, 1968), p. 554.

48. Gregory Baum, "The New Encyclical on Contraception," *Homiletic and Pastoral Review* 68 (September, 1968), p. 1003.

49. Baum, *Homiletic and Pastoral Review, op. cit.,* p. 1002.

50. Baum, *Commonweal, op. cit.,* p. 553.

51. Baum, *Homiletic and Pastoral Review, op. cit.,* p. 1004.

XI THE LAITY AND THE ENCYCLICAL

The two previous chapters attempted to summarize comments on the encyclical offered by national conferences of bishops and a number of well-known theologians. This chapter concerns the reactions of the laity.

The term "laity," used here to designate all those who do not belong to the hierarchy or to the community of professional theologians, embraces a wide variety of people who find themselves affected by the papal teaching in either their professional or personal lives, or both. Among them would be experts in the fields of philosophy, medicine, psychology, sociology, demography, and marriage counselling. It would include also the "rank and file" of the Church's membership, especially those most deeply touched by the encyclical's teaching—married couples.

The reactions of the laity, as in the case of the bishops and the theologians, were by no means uniform. They ranged from opposition and criticism through disappointment and resignation to complete, grateful acceptance and spirited, scholarly defense. There was also the unsophisticated smugness of the Brazilian taxi-cab driver who, when informed by a passenger that the Pope had banned the pill, remarked, "They should never have told him about it."[1] The places where these reactions appeared were many and varied: articles in books and scholarly journals, letters to the editors of countless newspapers and magazines, man-in-the-street interviews conducted by radio and television stations.

The lay reactions to *Humanae Vitae* present a new phenomenon in the Church—the laity talking back to the hierarchy, expressing their views on a theological issue and, in many cases at least, doing it in theological terms. Norman St. John-Stevas sees this new phenomenon as a sign of maturity in the Catholic laity. They have come of age in the Church, and feel it their right and duty to express what they think and how they feel. "Slaves prostrate themselves before their masters; sons, when they are of age, sometimes stand up in the household and contradict their father. This is not a mark of insolence but of maturity."[2]

It is this desire on the part of the laity to exercise their newly found maturity in the Church which is at the heart of the present dispute. "The laity of the Church has come of age, they are expressing their minds to the Holy Father. This is an act of love and trust, not of contumely and insult."[3]

An overall view of the lay response to the encyclical would seem to indicate that the publication of *Humanae Vitae* has produced little change in mentality on the part of the vast majority. Those who believed prior to the encyclical that contraception was wrong accepted *Humanae Vitae* as a vindication of their position. Those who had before favored the use of contraceptives found little in the papal teaching to move them to change their minds. Indeed, the publicity surrounding the encyclical and the reactions to it seem to have led to a heightened interest in the birth control issue, with reaffirmation in some countries of governmental policies promoting birth control, and a wider dissemination of birth control information. It is reported that many Portuguese women, who before the encyclical had never heard of the pill, were now eagerly trying to find out more about it![4]

IN SUPPORT OF THE ENCYCLICAL

Much of the support of the encyclical among the laity came from those who had always seen the Church as a symbol of stability and changelessness in the midst of a changing world. They had come to feel that the spirit of *aggiornamento,* sweeping so relentlessly through the Church, was robbing them of the age-old certainties which up to now they had always looked to the Church to defend. For them the uncompromising moral stand taken by the Pope in the encyclical was a balm offering relief and reassurance. Typical of this attitude was a letter to the editor of the *London Times,* which said:

The Pope's reaffirmation of the Church's teaching on contraception has been received by some Catholics with relief. The Church's teaching on faith and morals is immutable. . . . No amount of commissions, advisors, or even a large majority of people in favor of a change could give the Pope any authority to change the Church's doctrine.[5]

Indeed, had the Pope taken a stand different from the one adopted in the encyclical, this would have shaken the faith of those who were convinced that the condemnation of contraception could not be changed because it was a part of the Church's teaching on faith and morals. As one writer to the *London Tablet* expressed it:

I defend with joy and energy and without qualification the thesis that the Church has never changed her teaching on any matter of faith or morals and never can. If She were to do so, I would at once cease to be a Catholic, for by that act she would have shown her unique claim to be false.[6]

In a similar vein, a London resident wrote to the *London Times:*

For my wife (a graduate in history) and myself (in classics and law) the Pope's pronouncement has come as a relief and a reassurance. Had the decision been the reverse of this, the "crisis of conscience" facing many of our fellow Catholics would have been ours—no less real because it would have been less fashionable.[7]

It was not only Roman Catholics who endorsed the Pope's stand on the immutability of the moral law. One writer to the *London Times,* who described himself as an Anglican in his religious affiliation and a Conservative in his political philosophy, expressed his admiration that the Pope did not believe that all teachings need change with the times. He wrote: "It is refreshing to see that the Roman Catholic Church believes that principles are more important than popularity. Time will show that the firm stand the Church has taken on contraception is the right one."[8]

Another writer, identifying himself as "a younger member of the Anglican Church," gave "a warm welcome" to the Pope's statement:

It seems to me that we all too often lose sight of the fact that moral standards are absolute. There is a dangerous attitude abroad today which claims that if majority practice rejects some previously established moral standard, then it is ethical teaching which must be thrown overboard. To my mind it is this shamefaced retreat in the face of an increasingly permissive society which has led to the undermining of moral authority in this country.[9]

In the midst of the moral bankruptcy increasingly being created by an overly permissive society, the Pope's firm stand on the moral law was lauded by many as a desperately needed defense of the dignity of man and the sanctity of marriage. Malcolm Muggeridge, a broadcaster for the British Broadcasting Corporation (BBC), wrote to the *London Times:*

I do not doubt that in the history books when our squalid moral decline is recounted, with the final breakdown in law and order that must follow (for without a moral order there can be no social, political or any other order), the Pope's courageous and just, though I fear . . . largely ineffectual stand will be accorded the respect and admiration it deserves.[10]

Another writer to the *Times* says that what the encyclical represents is a necessary, though admittedly difficult call to discipline and restraint in the face of the all too prevalent hedonistic tendencies at loose in the contemporary world.

In an age where permissiveness is eating away at the roots of the nations' lives, where sex is shamelessly exploited in the mass media of the day and the pill itself discussed and peddled as if it were some form of detergent . . . for the Church to relax her teaching on birth control would be to associate herself (however indirectly) with these unsavory trends.[11]

There were those, too, whose support of the encyclical was an expression of their loyalty to the Pope as the Vicar of Christ. They equated acceptance or rejection of the encyclical with acceptance or rejection of his authority. "Your Church is like your country. You don't desert it when things get rough. If the Pope says no pill, it's no pill for me."[12]

According to L. Brent Bozell, editor of the American magazine *Triumph,* those priests who refused to accept the encyclical had already placed themselves in a state of schism. They should leave the Church, for they can no longer claim to represent the Church if they refuse submission to an authoritative teaching of the Supreme Pontiff on faith and morals.[13]

Dietrich von Hildebrand

In much the same vein Dietrich von Hildebrand wrote: "If anyone assumes that the Pope is wrong and he knows better, he is clearly disavowing his belief in the teaching authority of the Church in morals and thereby ceases to be an authentic Catholic."[14]

One of the most spirited defenses of the encyclical came from this octogenarian philosopher, whose writings in the twenties and thirties, it will be remembered, had helped to give a change of direction to Catholic thinking on the meaning of Christian marriage. Von Hildebrand sees the central teaching of the encyclical—the inseparable link between the love-union of marriage and procreation—as a vindication of the approach to marriage that he had defended for so many years. For him there are two fundamental ways in which the dignity of marriage can be violated: (1) by the separation of the conjugal act from mutual love and from its context in marriage, and (2) by the active, artificial separation of the conjugal act from the possible generation of a human being. The first is the sin of impurity; but the second—the evil inherent in contraceptive intercourse—is a sin of irreverence because "it artificially cuts off the creative intervention of God, or better still, it artificially separates an act which is ordained toward cooperation with the creative act of God from this its destiny."[15]

At heart, such irreverence is a denial of man's creaturehood; it means that man is acting as if he were his own God. "It is the same sinfulness that lies in suicide or in euthanasia,"[16] in both of which man acts as if he were master of life.

Von Hildebrand, though, sees a decisive difference between contraception and the practice of rhythm. The intention of avoiding children is not in itself an act of irreverence; in fact serious reasons may fully justify such an intention. Nor, when serious reasons for avoiding offspring are present, is there any malice involved in limiting intercourse to the "God-given infertile period." Indeed, the fact that God has linked the conjugal act to the creation of a man during only relatively brief intervals is itself a sign of the order of things ordained by God. This "not only confirms that the bodily union of the spouses has a meaning and value in itself apart from procreation, but it also leaves open the possibility of avoiding conception, if this is desirable for serious reasons."[17]

The sin of contraception, therefore, consists precisely in the active, artificial severing of the mystery of bodily union from procreation at the time of possible fertility, i.e., at the time when they are linked together by the design of the Creator. "Only in this artificial intervention, where one *acts against* the mystery of superabundant finality, is there the sin of irreverence—that is to say, the sin of presumptuously exceeding the creatural rights of man."[18]

In answer to those who charge that the moral teaching of the encyclical is based on a biologism that subordinates personal values to an order that is merely biological, von Hildebrand agrees that personal values must always rank higher than biological ones. But he maintains that although the creation of a human person by God through the cooperation of a married couple requires certain biological conditions, it is never in itself merely a biological occurrence.

The fact that biological laws connect the conjugal act with the creation of a human person does not justify our considering the rupture of the connection only a biological intervention. An extreme case makes this immediately clear: a fatal shot through a man's head is not simply a "biological intervention" but a murder, because a man's life was connected with the physiological processes that were frustrated.[19]

Von Hildebrand also rejects, as does the encyclical, the argument that married couples sometimes find themselves in a situation in which the best they can do is choose the lesser of two evils. In other words, they must choose to practice contraception or risk the greater evil of endangering the stability and happiness of their marriage. Von Hildebrand does not accept the presupposition of this argument; he denies that harming a marriage could ever be a greater evil than using contraceptives because the latter is a moral evil, whereas the former is a "misfortune."

We are never allowed to do something morally evil in order to prevent a misfortune. Sins, which offend God, and great misfortunes (the destruction of high values through no moral fault of ours) are absolutely incomparable. Sin alone offends God; no misfortune—however great—is commensurate with the fearful disharmony issuing from an offense of God.[20]

DISAGREEMENT WITH THE ENCYCLICAL

Although many Catholics welcomed the Pope's statement on contraception as a sign of the Church's fidelity to her past tradition, many more found the encyclical disappointing and disturbing. They felt it set the Church at odds with what thoughtful, educated people throughout the world regarded as desirable and even necessary for the well-being of the human race and, further, signalled a retreat from the spirit of Vatican II. The preparation of the encyclical showed little evidence of collegial cooperation within the Church; the reasoning employed in it largely ignored the theological climate that had been in the process of development over several decades, and the conclusions drawn were seemingly in conflict with the life-experience of many deeply committed married people.

THE ENCYCLICAL AND THE PAPAL
BIRTH CONTROL COMMISSION

Many expressed serious concern that the encyclical rejected the views of the papal birth control commission without making any serious effort to refute them. Not unexpectedly, this concern was voiced by the members of the commission itself.

Dr. John Marshall, one of the original members appointed by Pope John XXIII, remarks that the members of the commission studied and gathered data for several years, and concluded from what they had learned that "they could not demonstrate the intrinsic evil of contraception on the basis of natural law."[21] Even the minority members of the commission admitted that this could not be done. But though the majority decided that for this reason the Church's teaching was open to change, the minority fell back on authority as the basis for continuing the traditional teaching of the Church.

The commission's report to the Pope, urging a change in the Church's teaching, was important, Dr. Marshall maintains, not simply because it reflected the thinking of the majority, but because it set forth the accumulated evidence that had moved the majority to take the stand that it did. The commission, he says:

. . . did not "vote" in the ordinary sense; they were not there to support a position; they were there to discover the truth insofar as they could, which for some resulted in a slow and painful change in the light of what was found. It was the weight of evidence discovered by the work of the commission, not the counting of heads, that was the subject of the report to the Holy Father.[22]

Apparently the weight of evidence amassed by the commission had little influence on the actual writing of *Humanae Vitae,* for the encyclical declares that there had emerged from the commission certain criteria for resolving the birth control question that "departed from the moral teaching on marriage proposed with constant firmness by the teaching authority of the Church";[23] for this reason these criteria could not be accepted. This statement seems to discount entirely the findings of the commission; yet the encyclical not only makes no effort to disprove these criteria, but fails even to designate them. Dr. Marshall reasons that the encyclical could scarcely have intended to include among these criteria the commission's conclusion that contraception was not intrinsically evil, for the question of whether it was or was not was the very one that the commission had been called together to study. What, then, were these criteria which the Pope felt compelled to reject? The failure of the encyclical to specify them has created a theological impasse because, if unaware of what these criteria are, "theology cannot advance without being in danger of falling into the same alleged errors."[24]

Dr. André E. Hellegers, a member of the papal commission who had assisted Father de Riedmatten in the secretarial work, sees a deeper problem in this rejection, without any attempt at refutation of the criteria proposed by the commission's experts. To him this can only mean that "the scientific method of inquiry is irrelevant to Roman Catholic theology."[25]

He says further:

It is made clear that nothing that a present or future scientist could possibly contribute in terms of scientific data could have any pertinence to the subject, if certain criteria of solution would emerge which depart from the moral teaching on marriage proposed with constant firmness by the teaching authority of the Church.[26]

The position taken in *Humanae Vitae,* therefore, not only hampers the work of theology but seems to nullify the very purpose of the papal commission's formation, since the teaching proposed with constant firmness by the Church was well known before the commission was appointed. What was the point in bringing together several dozen consultants if their findings were to be judged *a priori* in terms of their conformity to the teachings of the past? If the encyclical had declared that the data advanced by the commission were "wrong or irrelevant or insufficient to warrant a change in teaching,"[27] this would at least have been a position understandable to a scientist, even though he disagreed with it. But to restrict the function of the scientist to bringing forth data that would confirm the teaching of the past and to reject any data that he might propose solely because it conflicted with that teaching is simply "the antithesis of scientific procedure."[28]

Both Dr. Marshall and Dr. Hellegers disassociate themselves from the papal encyclical's statement that artificial birth control opens a wide and easy road towards conjugal infidelity and a general lowering of morality, and may even cause men to consider their wives as mere instruments of selfish enjoyment. Both contend that there is no scientific evidence to support this sociological assertion. Moreover, Dr. Marshall charges, it "casts a gratuitous slur, which I greatly regret, on the countless responsible married people who practice contraception and whose family life is an example to all."[29]

Mr. and Mrs. Patrick Crowley, also members of the papal commission, commented briefly on the encyclical. All that they were willing to say about it was that they welcomed Msgr. Lambruschini's comment that it was not an infallible or irreformable document. They were unhappy that the Pope had listened only to a small minority on the commission and expressed their disappointment that the encyclical seemed, to them at least, to be largely negative in tone at a time when—as the commission itself had so earnestly suggested—there was such need for "a more positive pedagogy on marriage."[30] They also were "not at all enthused by the emphasis on rhythm"[31] presented in the encyclical. On the basis of their own research into the practice of rhythm, the results of which they had presented to the commission, they had come to entertain grave doubts about its practicality "from the physiological, psychological and so many other aspects."[32]

Dr. John T. Noonan, a consultant to the papal commission though not a member, declared that the encyclical "suffers from both internal inconsistency and from inadequate preparation."[33] It is internally inconsistent because its central teaching that each and every marriage act must remain "open to the transmission of life" is in direct contradiction to the teaching that "the rhythm system of contraception may be used for appropriate reasons."[34] In addition, the encyclical, written by a handful of men, was inadequately prepared.

It is, to say the least, surprising that what is alleged to be the design of God could only be discovered in the utmost secrecy of a military character and without subjecting the statement of the alleged design of God to the scrutiny of the moral theologians who are experts in the matter or the comment of the faithful who would be expected to carry out the orders given.[35]

Internal Inconsistency

Dr. Noonan was by no means alone in charging the encyclical with internal inconsistency. The same fault seemed evident to Mr. O. A. Spencer, a Catholic family man and for more than twenty years an economic advisor to the governments of British Guiana, Malaya and the Sudan. Mr. Spencer found it impossible to reconcile the encyclical's condemnation of "every action which . . . whether as an end or as a means . . . renders procreation impossible" with its invitation to scientists to find means of making the "safe period" really safe. Making the safe period really safe would unquestionably be a means of rendering procreation impossible and as such, would therefore seem to have come under the ban laid down in the encyclical. Yet such an endeavor, far from being forbidden, is actually encouraged in *Humanae Vitae.* "I know," Dr. Spencer says, "that I shall be told that in the one case the means are 'natural' and in the other 'unnatural,' but, apart from being unable to see how the choice of a natural means legalizes an illegitimate action, I do not find the distinction itself logical."[36]

He points out that the variations in the feminine ovulatory cycle are "normal statistical variations around an observed norm";[37] as such they must be considered part of the nature of things.

To interfere with them, therefore, not for the purpose of promoting health, but to prevent conception by making a particular "safe-period" really safe, is just as much a contraceptive intervention in the total or normal conjugal situation of that couple as an intervention designed to defer temporarily male or female fertility.[38]

Michael Novak makes much the same point. Time, he argues, is as much a dimension of nature as is space.

I do not understand why it is "unnatural" to block the spatial flow of the sperm so that it does not fertilize an ovum . . . and yet not "unnatural" to time the placement of the sperm so that it does not fertilize an ovum. In either case human intelligence is directing the process so that the ovum will not be fertilized. In the first case a physical spatial object is inserted in the process; in the second case an equally physical temporal gap is deliberately . . . inserted in the process. I do not understand why spatial objects are blameworthy, while temporal gaps are not. Both are equally "natural" (or "unnatural").[39]

Furthermore, Mr. Novak says, infertility is as natural for a woman as fertility; she is, in fact, infertile for more days of the month than she is fertile. Fertility is realized in a particular act of intercourse "only when a whole series of physiological conditions are in a certain configuration."[40] Why, he asks, is that configuration an especially privileged one? Are not other configurations equally natural? Why is it good to use human art to enhance a woman's fertility, yet wrong to use that same art to enhance her infertility?

Dr. André Hellegers also finds inconsistent the fact that the encyclical calls upon the scientific community to perfect the rhythm method, yet at the same time charges married couples to keep each and every act of intercourse open to the transmission of life. What does it mean to perfect the rhythm method? Presumably it means to work toward a point where there would be 100 per cent assurance that a given act of sexual union would not lead to the birth of a child.[41] But even if rhythm were so perfected, it would still be necessary, if one is to abide by the teaching of the encyclical, to say that an act of intercourse during the safe period in such a situation of "perfect rhythm" would nevertheless be open to the transmission of life. This would simply create a language problem, for it would be saying that an act, scientifically 100 per cent closed to the transmission of life, is simultaneously "open to the transmission of life." In such a context the phrase "open to the transmission of life" would seem devoid of any real meaning.

Some lay writers professed to see yet another inconsistency in *Humanae Vitae's* recommendation that those who have been practicing contraception and find themselves unable to break that habit should have frequent recourse to the sacrament of Penance.

Is it seriously suggested that Catholics using contraceptives should go to Confession, be absolved, and then immediately return to the use of contraceptives? Such a situation, far from strengthening respect for spiritual authority, would radically undermine it. Catholics today do not require compassion in the confessional . . . but freedom and responsibility.[42]

The Encyclical and the Human Condition

Perhaps the most persistent complaint of laymen who commented adversely on the encyclical was that it did not seem to be attuned to the human condition in the contemporary world. Norman St. John-Stevas charges that it attempts to turn back the clock.

Brutally and blandly it brushes aside the whole development of Catholic thought on birth control which has taken place since the calling of the Council. It affirms as a fact a natural law position which had been rejected by many of the best minds in the Church and gives no justification for doing so. It ignores the fact that once freedom of discussion was gained within the Church the traditional position was exposed as riddled with contradictions and unproved assumptions.[43]

Others scored the encyclical for its failure to show any adequate concern for the demographic problems that have become a serious issue for the future good of humanity. Dr. Anthony Storr writes:

In 1965 world food production increased by one percent, but world population increased by two percent. Every day twice as many people are born as die. Our eyes are perpetually assailed and our hearts torn by press photographs of starving children. Yet the Pope forbids any method of contraception except one which is notoriously unreliable. I should not be able to sleep easily at night if I had his latest edict upon my conscience.[44]

A group of sixty Catholic psychologists, attending the national convention of the American Psychological Association in San Francisco, expressed their concern that the encyclical seemed to be out of touch with the scientific findings made available by contemporary psychology. It reflects, they say, an inadequate comprehension of the psychology of man and woman. Furthermore, by its failure to integrate into its teaching the latest scientific findings about man, the encyclical shows no sensitivity to the dilemma in which it places Catholic men of science.[45]

Much the same thing, though from a different point of view, was said by Robert Nowell, editor of *Herder Correspondence:* "With [its] analysis of married love there can be little, if any, disagreement; the tragedy is that it does not seem to have been allowed to affect the thinking to be found elsewhere in the encyclical."[46]

The encyclical, he goes on to say, makes a truly radical break with the classical doctrine that isolated the procreation and education of children as the primary end of marriage. It seems to express the contemporary understanding that procreation is an almost necessary by-product of married love. When a man and woman fall in love and decide to marry, they do not think primarily of having children. They think of living their lives together, and a natural part of living together is having children.

There is normally no question of excluding the idea of having children— indeed for a woman one aspect of being in love with a man is normally a desire to bear his children—but from a purely existential point of view it can hardly be described as the primary end of marriage. Procreation thus forms part of the total end of marriage, but it should not be isolated as if it alone were the major determining factor.[47]

The difficulty, Mr. Nowell suggests, is that this view of marriage—which can be found in Article 9 of the encyclical—seems to have been completely lost sight of when the moral problems related to birth regulation are discussed. The question of responsible parenthood is resolved in terms of the parents' duty to respect the functions of biological processes in marriage. The personalist dimension of married love is allowed to recede into the background and the tyranny of biological processes takes over.

Robert Hoyt, editor of the *National Catholic Reporter,* contends that this approach makes many people wonder whether the decision embodied in the encyclical, despite conscious efforts to incorporate a new dimension of conjugal love into it, is not in fact "rooted in a distrust of sex, an attitude which regards the use of sex even in marriage as a concession to man's animal nature and to the necessities of procreation."[48]

Many would ask, with Michael Novak, whether the Pope and his advisors are really aware of the human suffering and the sense of unreality involved in their concept of the meaning of sexuality in marriage.[49] Does the encyclical ignore, in the practical directives it issues, the deep significance of marital intercourse in the personal growth of husband and wife? Is it at all sensitive to the threat that its directives pose for family life and family stability? Do these directives really help to enhance the dignity of women—and no one can doubt that this was the Pope's intention—or do they in fact make it more difficult for a woman to achieve her essential dignity and growth as a person? "What," asks one mother, "can more surely enslave a woman than frequent pregnancies over which she herself is allowed no control?"[50]

This chapter has attempted to offer a representative sampling of lay responses to *Humanae Vitae.* Since these responses were so many and so varied, it would be presumptuous to attempt a summary or to suggest any definitive conclusions. This much at least can be said: The silence of centuries has been broken; the voice of the laity has at last been spoken in the Church. The question that only the future can answer is: To what extent will the voice of the laity be heard? To what extent will it contribute to a better understanding of God's will in the Church?

NOTES

1. "Latin America and South Europe," *New York Times,* August 18, 1968.

2. Norman St. John-Stevas, Letter to the Editor, *London Times,* August 5, 1968.

3. *Ibid.*

4. Edward B. Fiske, report in the *New York Times,* August 18, 1968.

5. Letter to the Editor, *London Times,* August 13, 1968.

6. Letter to the Editor, *London Tablet,* September 14, 1968.

7. M. T. Bushell, Letter to the Editor, *London Times,* August 1, 1968.

8. Geoffrey Baber, Letter to the Editor, *London Times,* August 1, 1968.

9. Robert Spooner, Letter to the Editor, *London Times,* August 1, 1968.

10. Malcolm Muggeridge, Letter to the Editor, *London Times,* August 2, 1968.

11. D. G. Galvin, Letter to the Editor, *London Times,* August 1, 1968.

12. Interview in Washington, D.C., reported in the *Rochester Times Union,* July 31, 1968.

13. L. Brent Bozell, *National Catholic Reporter,* August 7, 1968.

14. Dietrich von Hildebrand, *The Encyclical Humanae Vitae—A Sign of Contradiction* (Chicago: Franciscan Herald Press, 1969), p. 80.

15. *Op. cit.,* p. 37.

16. *Op. cit.,* p. 35.

17. *Op. cit.,* p. 47.

18. *Ibid.*

19. *Op. cit.,* p. 45.

20. *Op. cit.,* p. 70.

21. John Marshall, "The Council and the Commission," *London Tablet,* September 21, 1968.

22. *Ibid.*

23. Paul VI, *Humanae Vitae,* Art. 6.

24. John Marshall, *op. cit.*

25. André E. Hellegers, "A Scientist's Analysis," in Charles E. Curran, ed.,

Contraception: Authority and Dissent (New York: Herder & Herder, Inc., 1969), p. 217.

26. *Op. cit.*, p. 216.

27. *Op. cit.*, p. 217.

28. *Ibid.*

29. John Marshall, Letter to the Editor, *London Times,* July 31, 1968.

30. Patrick Crowley, *National Catholic Reporter,* August 7, 1968.

31. *Ibid.*

32. *Ibid.*

33. John T. Noonan, *National Catholic Reporter,* August 7, 1968.

34. *Ibid.*

35. *Ibid.*

36. O. A. Spencer, Letter to the Editor, *London Times,* August 8, 1968.

37. *Ibid.*

38. *Ibid.*

39. Michael Novak, "Frequent, Even Daily Communion," in Daniel Callahan, ed., *The Catholic Case for Contraception* (New York: The Macmillan Company, 1969), p. 94.

40. *Op. cit.*, p. 95.

41. Hellegers, *op. cit.*, p. 231.

42. Norman St. John-Stevas, Letter to the Editor, *London Times,* July 31, 1968.

43. *Ibid.*

44. Anthony Storr, Letter to the Editor, *London Times,* August 1, 1968.

45. "Psychologists Question Encyclical's Reasoning," *The* (Davenport) *Catholic Messenger,* September 12, 1968.

46. Robert Nowell, "Sex and Marriage," in *On Human Life* (London, Burns & Oates, 1968), p. 54.

47. *Ibid.*

48. Hoyt, *The Birth Control Debate,* p. 210.

49. Michael Novak, in Hoyt, *The Birth Control Debate,* p. 201.

50. Anne Marie Mutton, Letter to the Editor, *London Times,* August 1, 1968.

XII REFLECTIONS ON THE LIVELY DEBATE

Pope Paul, in his letter to the Congress of German Catholics on August 30, 1968, expressed the following hope: "May the lively debate aroused by our encyclical lead to a better knowledge of God's will."[1] It is worth noting that the Pope's statement makes the debate aroused by the encyclical, and not the encyclical itself, the basis of this hope.

The entire Catholic community shares this hope with Pope Paul. Yet for different people in that community this hope signifies different things. For some it may be the hope that dissenters from the encyclical will discover the will of God by accepting the decision of the magisterium. Others may hope that the authority of the Church will discover the will of God by giving in to dissent.

Such an either-or resolution of the tension that continues in the Church would seem to be neither realistic nor even desirable. It is unrealistic to expect the magisterium to change its position simply because there have been dissenting voices; Pope Paul, since the publication of the encyclical, has repeatedly insisted that the teaching he presented was not human but divine law. It is equally unrealistic to expect that the theological and pastoral climate that has become so widespread in the Church can be easily reversed. The fact that the controversy on birth control has continued unabated since the publication of the encyclical is an indication that such a reversal is not about to take place in the Church.

Resolution by capitulation—one way or the other—does not seem to be desirable either. It would mean a failure to face honestly issues that have been brought to the surface by the theological debates of the last decade—issues deeper than birth control alone. Capitulation would leave these issues unfaced and unresolved. In the long run this would do greater harm to the Church.

THE FUNCTIONING OF AUTHORITY IN THE CHURCH

Among these deeper issues, the most important perhaps is the functioning of authority in the Church, which was highlighted, significantly, by the first episcopal reaction to the encyclical—the joint letter of the Dutch bishops. The bishops conclude their statement with these words: "May the discussion on the papal letter contribute to a better and better functioning of authority within the Church."[2] The bishops state the issue most clearly. The question is not whether authority exists in the Church or whether its function is important. The crucial question is how it can best function and thus, in the most effective way possible, serve the good of the Church.

An answer to this question demands the facing up to other questions. How is the exercise of the Supreme Magisterium of the Church related to the teaching office of the world episcopate? How is the teaching office of both Pope and bishops related to the experience of the whole Church in its efforts to live the Gospel?

There are many in the Church today who, though unwilling to dispute the Pope's right to decide the birth control issue unilaterally, are nevertheless asking whether or not he should have done so. Could there not have been a better way for authority to function?

Archbishop Denis Hurley of Durban, South Africa, pointing to the "magnificent results achieved in the Council" through "full and open debate," declared that the Council was "collegiality at its finest, or almost finest, for the method and scope of consultation can still be widened to include more of God's people, his clergy, religious, and laity."[3]

He adds, however, that "the consultation on birth control was not conducted in the same way."[4] The bishops were asked to submit their opinions and most of them did, but this was by no means the same thing as discussing the issue in full and open debate. Though he believes that the Pope had the right to reserve to himself the decision on birth control, Archbishop Hurley admits that he would be dishonest if he were to say that he agreed with "the method of consultation or the result."[5] He says that the bishops, as brothers of Pope Paul in the episcopate, "cannot shrink from the issue of how they think the authority of their senior brother should be exercised. To discuss it with him is not disloyalty. . . ."[6]

As Archbishop Hurley indicates, the question of episcopal collegiality is not the only point at issue, for even if that collegiality were to operate much more broadly in the Church than it does today, the question would still have to be asked: Can collegiality function in a way that best serves the good of the Church unless there is dialogue and consultation within the whole Church?

More and more we are coming to realize that man comes to know what it means to be a man by the experience of living his manhood, and that the Christian comes to know what the Gospel of Jesus Christ means from his efforts to live the Gospel. Can we any longer, then, mark an exclusive division in the Church between the *ecclesia docens* and the *ecclesia discens*? Is not the teaching Church also the learning Church? Must not all the members of the Church, including its official teachers, listen to the Spirit speaking to the whole Church? Must not the experience of the faithful in living the Gospel be taken more seriously as a *locus theologicus* for the magisterium in articulating its teaching?

Pre-Vatican II theology often interpreted the experience of the faithful in the light of the teachings of the magisterium, which was almost tantamount to saying that we know from the magisterium what the faithful ought to experience. Can we not say that there are times when the situation should be reversed so that the experience of the faithful will help to interpret the teachings of the magisterium? In order for God's will to be known in the Church, it is not enough simply for the magisterium to teach. If what the magisterium teaches is to be effective in clarifying the will of God, it must become a part of the living experience of the Church. Would this perhaps mean that the magisterium needs to evaluate its teaching in terms of the way in which that teaching is absorbed into the life-stream of the Church? That what is not absorbed will eventually be set aside— by the magisterium itself?

This is not to say that the teaching of the magisterium requires the prior assent of the faithful before it becomes binding. It is simply to say that mere intellectual or notional assent on the part of the faithful is not enough. It is possible for people, out of a sense of loyalty and obedience, to say Yes to things that they eventually find they cannot live with. Could not the inability of the Christian community to absorb a particular teaching into its living experience be a sign to the magisterium that the Spirit operating in the whole Church is saying that this teaching needs to be reevaluated? Vatican II teaches that "the body of the faithful as a whole, anointed as they are by the Holy One, cannot err in matters of belief."[7] Would it not be a corollary of this teaching that the body of the faithful cannot err, either, in what they find themselves unable to believe?[8]

If the "lively debate" aroused by the encyclical has revealed tensions in the Church between the teaching of the magisterium and the experience of many of the faithful, it may be that the Church will come to know God's will more fully, not by suppressing these tensions, but by living with them. It may also be that acknowledging that these tensions admit of no immediate solution will make the eventual solution more meaningful.

THE THEOLOGY OF DISSENT

Another issue opened up by the "lively debate" on the encyclical is one closely related to the problem of the proper functioning of authority in the Church: the question of the right of dissent. The birth control debate may well help us to develop a more sophisticated understanding of the place of dissent in the life of the Church and the role that it plays in the development of her doctrine.

That dissent has a legitimate place in the life of the Church can hardly be disputed. The theological manuals of the past,[9] the writings of a notable number of contemporary theologians, and the statements of several national hierarchies offer ample evidence that dissent is not only a right that may be exercised in the Church, but at times may become a duty that one must not shirk.

The right to dissent is probably best understood if it is seen as the necessary consequence of a proper understanding of the meaning of assent to non-infallible teachings. Assent to non-infallible teaching means more than merely having the general disposition to accept whatever the Church teaches (though such a disposition may be presumed to be present in a Catholic, believing as he does that the magisterium enjoys the assistance of the Holy Spirit). Assent is a specific act directed to a particular teaching. It is not an act of obedience to Church authority, for obedience is primarily an act of the will whereas assent is an act of the mind. It is a free act which involves the personal appropriation of a particular teaching whereby a person makes that teaching his own conviction.

Since non-infallible teaching has always carried within itself the possibility of error (otherwise there would be no distinction between infallible teaching and non-infallible teaching), a situation could arise in which a person, however strong his dispositions to the contrary, might find himself unable to assimilate a particular non-infallible teaching. Since the free act of assent is psychologically impossible in such a situation, the only alternative consistent with true freedom and personal integrity would be to dissent. Dissent, then, is not an act of disloyalty to the Church or a denial of the magisterium's right to teach. It is simply the inevitable consequence of the inability in a concrete instance to give one's assent to a specific teaching of the magisterium. It is the necessary corollary of true freedom of assent.

It is true that some theologians, though conceding the right of dissent in the Church, would like to draw a distinction between private and public dissent. They allow that a theologian may privately communicate his reasons for dissent to the Church authorities, or even to his colleagues, but they deny that he has the right to make public his disagreement with official Church teaching. Increasingly, however, contemporary theologians suggest that such a restriction, even if desirable, is a practical impossibility in an age of rapid and open communication. If dissent is to be allowed at all, it cannot be kept private. The alternative to public dissent would seem to be no dissent at all.

It would seem, then, that much can be said for the legitimacy of dissent in the Church, and for a dissent that is not only private but public. But a further question remains to be answered. What is the role of dissent in the life of the Church? Is it something to be tolerated because it cannot be suppressed or is it something that should be welcomed because it contributes to the good of the Church? In other words, granted that there is an adequate apologetic for dissent in the Church, can there also be a positive theology of dissent? Is it a healthy phenomenon in the life of the Christian community that not everything taught by the magisterium is greeted with tranquillity and general applause? Does dissent have a value for that community, offering for its well-being something important which it otherwise would not have? Do those who dissent from non-infallible teaching have something to say that is important for the whole Church, and especially for the magisterium, to hear?

These are important questions, if only because in the recent history of the Church they have not been faced. Dissent, at least in the past hundred years, has not had a happy history in the Church. The

Syllabus of Errors; the rigid restrictions placed on biblical scholars by the early twentieth century decrees of the Biblical Commission; the cloud of suspicion that hovered so long over such creative theologians as Yves Congar, Henri de Lubac, Teilhard de Chardin, Karl Rahner; recent episcopal overreaction in the dioceses of Washington and Buffalo to priests who expressed their disagreement with *Humanae Vitae*—all these are sufficient signs, that in modern times at least, divergence of opinion in the Church has seldom received a warm welcome.

A positive theology of dissent will have to be based on certain presuppositions. First, it will be necessary to admit that the Church's understanding of the Gospel and of the mystery of human existence is constantly in the process of growth and development. In every age men ask new questions of the Gospel about the meaning of Christian existence—questions that grow out of the concrete situation in which they find themselves. Because the questions are new, the answers are not always immediately available nor are they achieved without struggle. Only God is omniscient, and we must not make the mistake of thinking that He has shared this prerogative with the Church. We must not make the *a priori* assumption that Church authority will have immediately at hand all the answers to the questions facing men, or even that the answers it has are necessarily and always the best. Vatican II acknowledged this fact: "Let the layman not imagine that his pastors are always such experts that to every problem which arises, however complicated, they can readily give him a concrete solution."[10] In short, if we are to understand the role of dissent in the Church, we must admit that the Church simply does not possess at any one time the totality of truth in all its explicitness.

A second presupposition for a positive theology of dissent is the realization that the magisterium needs human as well as divine help in deepening its understanding of the faith by which the Church lives. It needs the help of all its members, and the members should feel obliged to offer this help, even if at times it is in the form of disagreement.

Indeed, if the teaching of the magisterium may be seen as a gift to the Christian community, articulating the faith of that community and calling for assent, is it not possible to look upon dissent as a gift also—a gift from the community to the magisterium, which calls for a hearing and acts as a corrective that will assist the magisterium in articulating more clearly and profoundly the faith of the Church? Is this not implied by Vatican II when it speaks of the right and duty of the laity to voice their opinions? It says: "An individual layman, by reason of the knowledge, competence, or outstanding ability which he may enjoy, is permitted and sometimes even obliged to express his opinion on things which concern the good of the Church."[11]

Again Vatican II speaks of freedom of inquiry and freedom of expression in the Church: "Let it be recognized that all the faithful, clerical and lay, possess a lawful freedom of inquiry and of thought, and the freedom to express their minds humbly and courageously about those matters in which they enjoy competence."[12]

Granting these presuppositions—that the magisterium does not possess instant truth and that the rest of the Church has something to contribute to the understanding of truth (even at times in the form of a corrective of the magisterium's vision), we may suggest certain benefits that can result from dissent, especially when it is welcomed as a gift and not merely tolerated as a regrettable necessity.

Open acceptance of responsible dissent within the Church will be good for the public image of the Church. In an age of pluralism, it will make clear that the unity of the Church need not be identified with a rigid uniformity that stamps out all divergent thinking (even when that thinking does not affect the substance of faith). In an age of democracy, it will show that democratic processes that make it possible for everyone to be heard are not incompatible with the fundamental nature of the Church. It will demonstrate the Church's regard for true freedom of assent. It will be a sign of maturity in the Church, saying to all the world that the Church does not place a premium on mere submission but, rather, welcomes the mature reflections of her members even when those reflections disagree with certain positions which She has taken.

Responsible dissent freely allowed in the Church will protect the Church authority from being isolated. Father John J. O'Callaghan expressed the feeling of many about *Humanae Vitae,* when he said: "The idea of Pope Paul, alone on the remote heights of teaching authority, agonizing over the [birth control] decision which only he must make, does not appeal to me."[13]

Nor does it appeal to many people. Listening to dissenting voices in the Church will help the magisterium to keep in touch with the real situations in which people live and, consequently, to know what people are really thinking and feeling, what teachings they are able to absorb, and what they find themselves unable to accept. In other words, it will acquaint the magisterium with the actual circumstances in which official teaching has to be presented and show the Church authorities the frame of mind and will to which that teaching must relate if it is to be credible.

Dissent responsibly voiced and heard without anxiety can be a source of knowledge and understanding for the magisterium, opening up insights to truth which simply would not be available otherwise. Dissent places at the service of the Church the considered reflections of sincere and loyal Christians—reflections that would be lost to the Church, with the consequent loss to the clarity and depth of her teaching, if dissent were not allowed.

There can be no doubt that the publication of *Humanae Vitae* and the lively debate it has engendered have precipitated a crisis in the Church. Yet it is important to fix clearly the precise nature of that crisis. It is not a crisis of faith, despite the fact that events of the past year have shaken the faith of many. Whether one accepts the encyclical without qualification or disagrees with certain aspects of it, no substantial element of Catholic faith is implicated.

Neither is the crisis primarily and directly one of obedience, for obedience can never be the immediate response to a teaching. Although it is true that a teaching about morals (and the teaching of *Humanae Vitae* obviously concerns a moral matter) does call for obedience to the directives that flow from that teaching, obedience nevertheless can come only after assent. To ask a person to obey the directives of a non-infallible teaching to which he finds himself unable to assent, is to ask him to compromise his own personal integrity.

What, then, is the present crisis in the Church? Can it not be said that ultimately it is an ecclesiological crisis involving the Church's own self-awareness? Vatican II, reading the signs of the times, has offered (though not in a completely unambiguous way) a new vision of the Church—a vision in which authority operates collegially and through dialogue, and in which all the Church's members are implicated in her total mission.

The Church which was given the vision of Vatican II, however, has yet to become the Church envisioned by Vatican II. The controversy over the birth control issue may well be the catalyst which will assist her to become what at Vatican II She recognized herself to be. This may be the way in which the hope expressed by Pope Paul—that the "lively debate" aroused by the encyclical may lead the whole Church to a better knowledge of God's will—will be fulfilled.

NOTES

1. Paul VI, message to the 82nd Katholikentag, the biennial Congress of German Catholics, *London Tablet,* September 14, 1968. Also N. C. News Service, September 7, 1968.

2. *New York Times,* August 3, 1968.

3. Dennis Hurley, interview in the *Southern Cross* (Capetown), quoted in the *London Tablet,* August 31, 1968.

4. *Ibid.*

5. *Ibid.*

6. *Ibid.*

7. *Lumen Gentium,* Art. 12.

8. In this connection it is interesting to quote a standard theology manual used in Catholic seminaries: "The Holy Spirit will bring it about that the Church will never fall into error because of an encyclical. More probably He will do this

by seeing to it that the head of the Church will not issue an erroneous statement. However, it is not absolutely out of the question that He will prevent the error by virtue of its being detected by the subjects [of the Pope] and their ceasing to give an internal assent." L. Lercher, *Institutiones Theologicae*, Vol. 1, sec. 499 (Barcelona, 1945), quoted in the *London Tablet*, September 14, 1968. Also see Joseph A. Komonchak, "Ordinary Papal Magisterium and Religious Assent," in Curran, *Contraception: Authority and Dissent*, p. 112.

9. For a study of the teaching of the theology manuals on the right of dissent, see the article of Joseph A. Komonchak in Curran, *Contraception: Authority and Dissent*, pp. 101–126.

10. *Gaudium et Spes,* Art. 43, par. 5.

11. *Lumen Gentium,* Art. 37, par. 1.

12. *Gaudium et Spes,* Art. 62, par. 9.

13. John J. O'Callaghan, "Reflections on *Humanae Vitae,*" *Theology Digest* 16 (Winter, 1968), p. 325.

BIBLIOGRAPHY

Adamo, S. J., "The Pill and the Press," *Camden Star Herald,* April 3, 1964.

Baum, Gregory, "Birth Control—What Happened?" *Commonweal* 83 (December 24, 1965), pp. 369–371.

———, "The Right to Dissent." *Commonweal* 88 (August 23, 1968), pp. 553–554.

———, "The New Encyclical on Contraception." *Homiletic and Pastoral Review* 68 (September, 1968), pp. 1001–1004.

Bekkers, W. M., *God's People on the March.* New York, Holt, Rinehart & Winston, Inc., 1966, pp. 1–180.

Birmingham, William, *What Modern Catholics Think About Birth Control.* Signet Books. New York, New American Library, 1964, pp. 1–256.

Broun, Heywood, and Leech, Margaret, *Anthony Comstock, Roundsman of the Lord.* New York, A. & C. Boni, 1927, pp. 1–285.

Brown, Robert McAfee, "The Rock Book—A Protestant Viewpoint." *Commonweal* 78 (July 5, 1963), pp. 395–397.

Burghardt, Walter J., "Freedom and Authority in Education." *Theology Digest* 16 (Winter, 1968), pp. 310–316.

Callahan, Daniel, ed., *The Catholic Case for Contraception.* New York, The Macmillan Company, 1969, pp. xvi–240.

Cardegna, Felix F., "Contraception, the Pill and Responsible Parenthood." *Theological Studies* 25 (December, 1964), pp. 611–636.

Cavanagh, John R., *The Popes, the Pill and the People.* Milwaukee, Bruce Publishing Co., 1964, pp. vii–128.

Chevalier, L. R., "The Secret Drama Behind the Pope's Momentous

Decision on Birth Control." *Ladies Home Journal* 83 (March, 1966), pp. 88–89

Connell, Francis J., "Answers to Questions." *American Ecclesiastical Review* 143 (September, 1960).

Connery, John R., "Notes on Moral Theology." *Theological Studies* 19 (December, 1958), pp. 533–571.

Crooker, Robert W., "Pastoral Directives of *Humanae Vitae*." *Homiletic and Pastoral Review* 69 (October, 1968), pp. 13–26.

Curran, Charles E., "Christian Marriage and Family Planning." *Jubilee* 12 (August, 1964), p. 8–13.

———, *Contraception, Authority and Dissent*. New York, Herder & Herder, Inc., 1969, p. 239.

Dennett, Mary Ware, *Birth Control Laws*. New York, Hitchcock, 1927, pp. 1–309.

Dingle, Reginald J., *Cardinal Bourne at Westminster*. London, Burns & Oates, 1934, pp. vii–192.

Dirks, Walter (Rev. Gregor Roy), "The Pope and the Church." *Cross Currents* 19 (Winter, 1969), pp. 1–11.

Doms, Herbert, *The Meaning of Marriage*. New York, Sheed and Ward, Inc., 1939, pp. xxiv–229.

Duhamel, Joseph S., "The Time Has Come." A review in *America* 108 (April 27, 1963), pp. 608–611.

Dulles, Avery, "Karl Rahner on 'Human Life'." *America* 119 (September 28, 1968), pp. 250–252.

Dummett, Michael, "The Documents of the Papal Commission on Birth Control." *New Blackfriars* 50 (February, 1969), pp. 211–250.

Dupré, Louis, *Contraception and Catholics*. Baltimore, Helicon Press, Inc., 1964, pp. 1–94.

———, "From Augustine to Janssens." *Commonweal* 80 (June 5, 1964), pp. 336–342.

———, "Toward a Reexamination of the Catholic Position on Birth Control." *Cross Currents* 14 (Winter, 1964), pp. 63–85.

———, "A Critique of the Argument against Contraception Presented by Grisez," *National Catholic Reporter*, April 28, 1965.

Farraher, Joseph J., "Notes on Moral Theology." *Theological Studies* 21 (December, 1960), pp. 581–625.

———, "Notes on Moral Theology." *Theological Studies* 22 (December, 1961), pp. 610–651.

Ford, John C., and Kelly, Gerald, *Contemporary Moral Theology,* Vol. 2. Westminster, Md., The Newman Press, 1964, pp. viii–474.

Gilby, Thomas, "The Encyclical Abstraction." *New Blackfriars* 50 (November, 1968), pp. 94–102.

Griese, Orville N., *The Morality of Periodic Continence.* Washington, D.C., Catholic University Press, 1943.

Grisez, Germain G., *Contraception and the Natural Law.* Milwaukee, Bruce Publishing Co., 1964, pp. xiii–245.

Haney, Robert W., *Comstockery in America.* Boston, Beacon Press, 1969, pp. 1–199.

Hardin, Garrett, ed., *Population, Evolution and Birth Control.* San Francisco, W. H. Freeman and Co., Inc., 1964, pp. 1–341.

Häring, Bernard, "On the Encyclical." *London Tablet,* September 21, 1968.

Harris, Peter, et. al., *On Human Life.* London, Burns & Oates, 1968, pp. 1–264.

Hoyt, Robert G., ed., *The Birth Control Debate.* Kansas City, National Catholic Reporter, 1968, pp. 1–224.

Janssens, Louis, "L'Inhibition de l'ovulation est-elle moralement licite?" *Ephemerides Theologicae Lovanienses* 34 (April-June, 1958), pp. 357–360.

———, "Morale conjugale et progestogenes." *Ephemerides Theologicae Lovanienses* 39 (October-December, 1963).

———, "Moral Problems Involved in Responsible Parenthood." *Louvain Studies* 1 (Fall, 1966), pp. 3–18.

Kelly, Gerald, "Notes on Moral Theology." *Theological Studies* 7 (1946), pp. 105–106.

———, "Contraception and Natural Law." *Proceedings of the Catholic Theological Society of America* (June, 1963), pp. 25–45.

———, "Notes on Moral Theology." *Theological Studies* 24 (December, 1963), pp. 626–651.

———, "Confusion: Contraception and the Pill." *Theology Digest* 12 (Summer, 1964), pp. 123–130.

Lader, Lawrence, *The Margaret Sanger Story.* New York, Doubleday & Co., Inc., 1955, pp. 1–352.

Lynch, John J., "Fertility Control and the Moral Law." *Linacre Quarterly* 20 (August, 1953), pp. 83–89.

———, "Another Moral Aspect of Fertility Control." *Linacre Quarterly* 20 (November, 1953), pp. 118–122.

———, "Moral Aspects of Pharmaceutical Fertility Control." *Proceedings of the Catholic Theological Society of America* (1958), pp. 127–138.

———,"Notes on Moral Theology." *Theological Studies* 23 (June, 1962), pp. 233–265.

———, "Notes on Moral Theology." *Theological Studies* 26 (June, 1965), pp. 242–279.

———, "Notes on Moral Theology." *Theological Studies* 27 (June, 1966), pp. 242–265.

———, "The Time Has Come." Book review in *Marriage* 45 (June, 1963), pp. 14–17.

Marshall, John, "The Council and the Commission." *London Tablet,* September 21, 1968.

McCabe, Herbert, "Contraceptives and Natural Law." *New Blackfriars* 46 (November, 1964), pp. 89–96.

McCormick, Richard A., "Anti-Fertility Pills." *The Homiletic and Pastoral Review* 62 (May, 1962), pp. 692–700.

———, "Whither the Pill?" *Catholic World* 199 (July, 1964), pp. 207–214.

———, "Notes on Moral Theology." *Theological Studies* 29 (December, 1968), pp. 679–741.

McReavy, L. L., "The Essential Doctrine of *Humanae Vitae.*" *Clergy Review* 53 (November, 1968), pp. 861–867.

———, "Use of Steroid Drugs to Regularize Menstrual Cycles." *Clergy Review* 46 (December, 1961), pp. 746–750.

Noonan, John T., Jr., *Contraception: A History of its Treatment by the Catholic Theologians and Canonists,* Cambridge, Mass., Harvard University Press, 1965, pp. x–561.

Novak, Michael, ed., *The Experience of Marriage.* New York, The Macmillan Company, 1964, pp. vii–173.

O'Callaghan, Dennis, "The Birth Control Crisis." *Catholic World* 204 (March, 1967), pp. 326–334. Reprinted from *Clergy Review* (November, 1966).

———, "Fertility Control by Hormonal Medication." *Irish Theological Quarterly* 27 (January, 1960), pp. 1–15.

O'Callaghan, John J. "Reflections on *Humanae Vitae*." *Theology Digest* 16 (Winter, 1968), pp. 317–327.

O'Connell, Hugh, "Is Rhythm per se Illicit?" *American Ecclesiastical Review* 119 (November, 1948), pp. 336–347.

O'Grady, Desmond, "Pontifical Commission." *National Catholic Reporter,* March 24, 1965.

O'Leary, Maurice, "Debates over Birth Control Clarified." *Catholic Herald,* April 24, 1964.

Padovano, Anthony T., "In Defense of the Encyclical." *Catholic World* 208 (December, 1968), pp. 112–116.

Paul VI, "Address to the Birth Control Group." *National Catholic Reporter,* April 7, 1965.

———, "Allocution to the Italian Society of Obstetrics and Gynecology." N.C.W.C. News Service November 7, 1966.

———, "*Humanae Vitae*." Washington, D.C., *United States Catholic Conference* (July 25, 1968).

Pius XII, "Apostolate of the Midwife." *Catholic Mind* (January, 1952).

———, "Morality in Marriage." *Catholic Mind* (May, 1952).

———, "Morality and Eugenics." *The Pope Speaks* 6 (December, 1960).

Pyle, Leo, ed., *The Pill and Birth Regulation.* Baltimore, Helicon Press, Inc., 1964, pp. 1–225.

Rahner, Karl, "Democracy in the Church." *Month* 40 (September, 1968), pp. 105–119.

———, "On the Encyclical *Humanae Vitae*." *Stimmen Der Zeit,* September, 1968. English translation by David E. Schlaver, *National Catholic Reporter,* September 18, 1968.

Ratner, Herbert, "The Rock Book—A Catholic Viewpoint." *Commonweal* 78 (July 5, 1963), pp. 392–395.

Reuss, J. M., "Mutual Love and Procreation." *Tubinger Theologischen Quartalshrift* 143 (1963), pp. 454–475.

Riga, Peter J., "Pope Paul's Encyclical on Birth Control." *Catholic World* 208 (December, 1968), pp. 107–111.

Roberts, Thomas D., ed., *Contraception and Holiness.* New York, Herder & Herder, Inc., 1964, pp. 1–346.

Rock, John, "We Can End the Battle over Birth Control!" *Good Housekeeping* (July, 1961), pp. 44–45; 107–110.

———, *The Time Has Come*. Avon Books. New York, Alfred A. Knopf, Inc., 1963, pp. 1–194.

Ruether, Rosemary, "Marriage, Love, Children." *Jubilee* 11 (December, 1963), pp. 17–20.

Rynne, Xavier, *The Fourth Session*. New York, Farrar, Straus & Giroux, 1966, pp. 1–368.

Sieve, Benjamin, "A New Anti-Fertility Factor." *Science* 116 (October 10, 1952), pp. 373–385.

Snoeck, André, "Fecondation inhibée et morale Catholique." *Nouvelle Revue Theologique* 75 (July-August, 1953), pp. 690–702.

Swift, Francis W., "An Analysis of the American Theological Reaction to Janssens' Stand on 'The Pill'." *Louvain Studies* 1 (Fall, 1966), pp. 19–53.

Van der Marck, W., *Love and Fertility*. London, Sheed & Ward Ltd., 1965, pp. 1–105.

Von Hildebrand, Dietrich, *The Encyclical Humanae Vitae—A Sign of Contradiction*. Chicago, Franciscan Herald Press, 1969, pp. xiv–89.

———, *In Defense of Purity*. New York, Sheed & Ward, Inc., 1935, pp. 1–196.

———, "Marriage and Overpopulation." *Thought* 36 (1961), pp. 81–100.

Ward, Maisie, *Be Not Solicitous*. New York, Sheed & Ward, Inc., 1953, pp. 1–254.

Members of the Pontifical Study
Commission on Family,
Population and Birth Problems

The Most Rev. Leo Binz, archbishop of St. Paul, Minnesota

The Most Rev. Joseph Reuss, auxiliary bishop of Mayence, Germany

Canon Paul Anciaux, professor of the major seminary of Malines, Belgium

Rev. Alfons Auer, professor of theology, Würzburg, Germany

Dr. Donald Barrett, professor of sociology, University of Notre Dame, Indiana

Dr. J. R. Bertolus, psychoanalyst, Paris, France

Dr. Thomas Burch, population expert, Georgetown University, Washington, D.C.

Dr. John R. Cavanagh, psychiatrist, professor, Catholic University of America, Washington, D.C.

Dr. Colin Clark, economist, professor, Oxford University, England

Prof. Bernardo Colombo, professor, Venice and Padua, Italy

Dr. Mercedes B. Concepcion, demographer, professor, University of the Philippines, Manila

Mr. and Mrs. Patrick Crowley, Christian Family Movement, Chicago, Illinois

Canon Philip Delhaye, Catholic theological faculty, University of Lille, France

Dr. Michael Dembélé, director of the Ministry of Planning, Dakar, Senegal

Dr. Manuel Diegues, Rio de Janeiro, Brazil

Dr. Anthony Feanny, Kingston, Jamaica

Dr. Jacques Férin, gynecologist, professor, University of Louvain, Belgium

Rev. John C. Ford, S.J., Catholic University of America, Washington, D.C.

Rev. Joseph Fuchs, S.J., Gregorian University, Rome, Italy

Dr. Marcel Gaudefroy, gynecologist, Lille, France

Rev. Tullo Goffi, seminary professor, Brescia, Italy

Prof. Albert Görres, professor of medicine and psychology, Frankfurt, Germany

Rev. Bernard Häring, C.SS.R., moral theologian, Rome, Italy

Dr. André E. Hellegers, gynecologist, Johns Hopkins University, Baltimore, Maryland

Msgr. George A. Kelly, director of the Family Life Bureau, New York, New York

Mrs. J. F. Kulanday, Public Health Department, New Delhi, India

Rev. Michel Labourdette, O.P., theologian, Toulouse, France

Msgr. Ferdinando Lambruschini, theologian, University of the Lateran, Rome, Italy

Rev. Louis Lebret, O.P., sociologist, Paris, France

Msgr. G. Lemaitre, president of the Pontifical Academy of Sciences, Louvain, Belgium

Rev. Stanislas de Lestapis, S.J., theologian, Paris, France

Canon Pierre de Locht, National Center of Family Pastoral Work, Brussels, Belgium

Prof. Juan Jose Lopez-Ibor, psychiatrist, University of Madrid, Spain

Msgr. Jean Margeot, vicar-general of the diocese of Port Louis, Mauritius

Dr. John Marshall, neurologist, University of London, England

Prof. A. Mattelart, sociologist, Catholic University of Santiago, Chile

Prof. André van Melsen, philosopher of science, Nijmegen, Holland

Rev. C. Mertens, S.J., population expert, Eegenhoven, Belgium

Prof. Jacques Mertens de Wilmars, economist, Louvain, Belgium

Dr. Henri Moins, Tunis, Tunisia

Dr. Paul Moriguchi, Tokyo, Japan

Rev. G. Perico, S.J., theologian, University of Milan, Italy

Dr. and Mrs. Laurent Potvin, Ottawa, Ontario

Dr. R. Rabary, Tananarive, Madagascar

Dr. J. Razafinbahiny, sociologist, Madagascar

Dr. and Mrs. Henri Rendu, Paris, France

Rev. Henri de Riedmatten, O.P., Geneva and Fribourg, Switzerland

Dr. P. van Rossum, Brussels, Belgium

Mr. John C. Ryan, demographer, Bangalore, India

Rev. J. Sasaki, demographer, University of Eichi, Osaka, Japan

Rev. Raymond Sigmond, O.P., Institute of Social Studies, *Angelicum,* Rome, Italy

Dr. Marcel Thibault, director of the Center of Zoological Research, Paris, France

Rev. Jan Visser, C.SS.R., theologian, Lateran University, Rome, Italy

Prof. Francesco Vito, rector of the University of the Sacred Heart, Milan, Italy

Rev. Marcelino Zalba, S.J., theologian, Gregorian University, Rome, Italy

Consultant: Dr. John T. Noonan, University of Notre Dame, Indiana

The Individual American Bishops
and the Encyclical—
"The Bishop Shannon Case"

In addition to having commented upon *Humanae Vitae* in the joint letter of the National Conference of Catholic Bishops, many American bishops spoke individually to their people of the encyclical through pastoral letters or articles in diocesan weeklies. For the most part, the statements were couched in general terms. The bishops asserted their loyalty to the Pope and admonished the faithful to accept wholeheartedly the teaching of the encyclical, but they showed little inclination to discuss in detail any of the encyclical's contents. Few were disposed to follow the lead of Cardinal Patrick O'Boyle of Washington, D.C., or of Bishop James A. McNulty of Buffalo, New York, by using canonical penalties or the "power of appointment" to bring into line priests who had expressed their disagreement with certain elements in the encyclical.

In fact, a meeting of the administrative board of the National Conference of Catholic Bishops, held in Washington on September 16–17, 1968, discussed and attempted to clarify the question of dissent in the Church. At this meeting Bishop Alexander M. Zaleski of Lansing, Michigan, chairman of the Bishops' Commission on Doctrine, presented a scholarly paper discussing the loyalty owed by Catholics to papal teaching and offered guidelines to be followed by a Catholic who believed that he must in conscience dissent from such teaching. The guidelines presented by Bishop Zaleski were the following:

1. It is possible that a person in good faith may be unable to give internal assent to an encyclical.

2. As a loyal son of the Church, such a person must beware of voicing his dissent in the wrong way.

3. Dissent can be expressed but it must be done in a manner becoming to a docile believer and loyal son of the Church.

4. Such dissent must show that it is an expression from a believing person, from a man of faith.

5. Such dissent can only be expressed in a manner which does not disturb the consciences of other believing people.

6. Dissent must be accompanied by an open mind and a willingness to alter one's view in the light of new evidence.

7. Such dissent must be brought to the proper authorities in the proper manner and quietly.[1]

At least one member of the American hierarchy made use of these guidelines in expressing his own dissent. James P. Shannon, Auxiliary Bishop of the archdiocese of St. Paul-Minneapolis, Minnesota, in a confidential letter to Pope Paul written on September 23, 1968, invoked the Zaleski guidelines to explain to the Holy Father why he could not "in conscience give internal assent, hence much less external assent"[2] to the papal teaching that "each and every marriage act (*quilibet matrimonii usus*) must remain open to the transmission of life."[3] Bishop Shannon stated that he had found this "rigid teaching" simply "impossible of observance by many faithful and generous spouses," and he could not believe that "God binds men to impossible standards."[4] In his efforts to keep faith with the Pope and at the same time with the people who sought his counsel, he found himself "resorting to all sorts of casuistry and devious kinds of rationalization." He added: "I must now reluctantly admit that I am ashamed of the kind of advice I have given some of these good people, ashamed because it has been bad theology, bad psychology, and because it has not been an honest reflection of my own inner conviction."[5]

Two months later, on November 23, Bishop Shannon submitted to his immediate superiors in the archdiocese, Archbishops Leo Binz and Leo C. Byrne, his resignation as auxiliary bishop and pastor of St. Helena's Church. Subsequently, he was called to Washington for an interview with the apostolic delegate, Archbishop Luigi Raimondi, who indicated that the Holy See would accept his resignation. He also offered to arrange an assignment for Bishop Shannon outside the United States, but Shannon eventually rejected this offer when, in a later interview with the apostolic delegate, it became clear that the assignment would involve no pastoral duties or canonical appointment, but would simply provide a place of residence.[6]

The facts of "the Bishop Shannon Case" did not become public knowledge until May 28, 1969, when the *Minneapolis Star,* in an article by its religion editor, Wilmar Thorkelson, broke the news of the Bishop's letter to the Pope and of his offer to resign.[7] Subsequent articles in *The Minneapolis Star,* the *National Catholic Reporter* and elsewhere have filled in the details of the picture.

On June 30 Bishop Shannon announced that he had accepted the post of vice-president at St. John's College in Santa Fe, New Mexico (where he had been teaching during the spring semester, while on leave of absence from his duties as auxiliary bishop). On August 2 he married Mrs. Ruth Church Wilkinson of Rochester, New York, in a ceremony performed at the First Christian (Disciples of Christ) Church in Endicott, New York. In a statement to the press following his marriage, Bishop Shannon said: "I do not intend to leave the Catholic Church. It is my spiritual home. I love it dearly and have worked to the best of my ability as one of its priests for twenty-three years."[8]

Many of Bishop Shannon's supporters expressed their disappointment, not so much at the decision he had made, but at the consequences it would have for the Church. His marriage, they felt, removed from the ecclesiastical scene a powerful leader in the cause of Church reform, a leader of whom Robert G. Hoyt of the *National Catholic Reporter* had said: "He has been the bishop who has made life tolerable for liberal Catholics in this country."[9]

NOTES

1. *National Catholic Reporter* (June 4, 1969).

2. *Ibid.*

3. Paul VI, *Humanae Vitae,* Art. 11.

4. *National Catholic Reporter* (June 4, 1969).

5. *Ibid.*

6. Interview with Bishop Shannon, *National Catholic Reporter* (August 20, 1969).

7. Wilmar Thorkelson, "Birth Issue Causes Bishop's Resignation," *The Minneapolis Star* (May 28, 1969).

8. *The* (Davenport) *Catholic Messenger* (August 14, 1969).

9. *New York Times* (May 29, 1969).